Just Listen 'n Learn
GREEK

Eleni Marcopoulos-Gambarotta

Jennifer Scamp

General editor, Brian Hill

Series advisers

Janet Jenkins
Duncan Sidwell
Al Wolff

PASSPORT BOOKS
a division of *NTC Publishing Group*
Lincolnwood, Illinois USA

Acknowledgments

We are grateful to the following for permission to reproduce copyright material:

R. Conway Morris for the photograph on page 188.

L. Kandaros for the photographs on pages 48, 52, 61, 76, 89, 92, 104, 105, 108, 125.

The National Tourist Organization of Greece for the photographs on pages 80, 90, 92, 145, 150, 160, 172, 180, 200, 206 and 212.

Our thanks to the Greek people who helped with the recordings in Greece and the Polytechnic of Central London for all studio recordings.

Tape production: Gerald Ramshaw
Acting: Alexandros Martin, Vasiliki Cawson, Dr A. Anagnostidis
Book design: Gillian Riley
Illustrations: Rowan Barnes-Murphy

Note on the Accompanying Recorded Material

The *Just Listen 'n Learn* Language Programs are available in either audiocassette or compact disc formats. References in this book to the taped or recorded material apply equally to the audiocassettes and compact discs.

1994 Printing

Contents

How to use this course

Following this course will help you understand, speak and read most of the Greek you are likely to need on vacation or on business trips. The course is based on recordings made in Greece of ordinary Greek people in everyday situations. Step by step you will learn first to understand what they are saying and then to speak in similar situations yourself.

Before producing the course we talked to hundreds of people about why and how they learn languages. We know how important it is for learning to be enjoyable – and for it to be usable as soon as possible. Again and again people told us that there was not much point in knowing all the grammar if you were unable to ask for a cup of coffee! The only explanations of grammar will be ones that actually help you understand and use the language.

In order to get you to practice speaking Greek as quickly as possible we have not used the Greek alphabet in the main part of the course. We do, however, introduce the letters of the alphabet gradually so that you will be able to read all the Greek letters by Unit 13.

You should keep in mind from the very beginning that stress – where you put the emphasis on each word – is extremely important in Greek. When you say Greek words, pronounce the stressed syllable as emphatically as possible; this may sound odd to your own ear at first but, in fact, it is impossible to overdo it. (In English stress is not as marked as in Greek, but you only have to say the noun 'a próject' and the verb 'to projéct' to hear it is there nonetheless.) In Greek the stress usually falls on the next-to-last syllable – where it does not we have marked it e.g. ti kánete? (how do you do?) and efharistó (thank you). Even if you pronounce a word correctly in Greek you will frequently not be understood if you do not put the stress in the right place. This would be the same in English if you were to say 'imporTANT' instead of IMPORTant'. Anyway don't worry about this too much: you will pick up the correct pronunciation and stress if you follow the dialogues on the tape closely.

General hints to help you use the course

- Have confidence in us! Real language is complex and you will find certain things in every unit which are not explained in detail. Don't worry about this. We will build up your knowledge slowly, selecting only what is most important to know at each stage.
- Try to study regularly, but in short periods. 20–30 minutes each day is usually better than 3½ hours once a week.
- To help you learn to speak, say the words and phrases out loud whenever possible.
- If you don't understand something, leave it for a while. Learning a language is a bit like doing a jigsaw or a crossword: there are many ways to tackle it and it falls into place eventually.
- Don't be afraid to write in the book and add your own notes.
- Do review frequently. (There are revision/review sections after every three units.) It helps to get somebody to test you – and they don't need to know
- Greek.
  If you can possibly learn with somebody else you will be able to help each other and practice the language together.
- Learning Greek may take more time than you thought. Just be patient and above all don't get angry with yourself.

Suggested study pattern

Each unit of the course consists of approximately fourteen pages in the book and ten minutes of tape. The first page of each unit will tell you what you are going to learn and suggest what we think is the best method for going about it. As you progress with the course you may find that you evolve a method of study which suits you better – that's fine, but we suggest you keep to our pattern at least for the first two or three units or you may find you are not taking full advantage of all the possibilities offered by the material.

The book contains step-by-step instructions for working through the course: when to use the book on its own, when to use the tape on its own, when to use them both together, and how to use them. On the tape our presenter Alexandros will guide you through the various sections. Here is an outline of the study pattern proposed.

Dialogues

Listen to the dialogues, first without stopping the tape, and get a feel for the task ahead. Then go over each one bit by bit in conjunction with the vocabulary and the notes. You should get into the habit of using the PAUSE/ STOP and REWIND buttons on your cassette recorder to give yourself time to think, and to go over the dialogues a number of times. Don't leave a dialogue until you are confident that you have at least understood it. (Symbols used in the notes are explained on p. 6)

Key words and phrases

Study this list of the most important words and phrases from the dialogues. If possible, try to learn them by heart. They will be practiced in the rest of the unit.

Practice what you have learned

This section contains a selection of exercises which focus your attention on the most important language in the unit. To do them you will need to work closely with the book and often use your tape recorder – sometimes you are asked to write an exercise and then check the answers on tape: other times to listen first and then fill in answers in the book. Again, use your PAUSE/ STOP and REWIND buttons to give yourself time to think and to answer questions. Pauses have been left to help you to do this.

Grammar

At this stage in a unit things should begin to fall into place and you are ready for the grammar section. If you really don't like grammar, you will still learn a lot without studying this part, but most people really enjoy finding out how the language they are using actually works and how it is put together. In each unit we have selected just one or two important grammar points.

The Greek alphabet and Did you know?

In these sections you will gradually build up a knowledge of the Greek alphabet and learn how to read the kind of signs, menus, brochures, and so on you may come across in Greece. You will also be given some practical background information on Greek customs and culture.

Your turn to speak

Finally, back to the tape for some practice in speaking the main words and phrases which you have already heard and had explained. The book only gives you an outline of the exercises, so you are just listening to the tape and responding. Usually you will be asked to take part in a conversation where you hear a question or statement in Greek; followed by a suggestion in English as to how you might reply. You then give your reply in Greek and listen to see if you were right. You will probably have to go over these spoken exercises a few times before you get them absolutely correct.

Answers   The answers to all the exercises (except those given on tape) can be found on the last page of each unit.

If you haven't learned languages using a tape before, just spend five minutes on Unit 1 getting used to the mechanics: practice pausing the tape, and see how long the rewind button needs to be pressed to recap on different length phrases and sections.

Don't be shy – take every opportunity you can to speak Greek to Greek people and to listen to real Greek. Try listening to Greek broadcasts on the radio.

Kalí epitihia

At the back of the book

Symbols and abbreviations

If your cassette recorder has a counter, set it to zero at the start of each unit and then fill in these boxes with the number showing at the beginning of each dialogue. This will help you find the right place on the tape quickly when you want to wind back.

♦   This indicates a key word or phrase in the dialogues.

m.	masculine	sing.	singular
f.	feminine	pl.	plural
n.	neuter	lit.	literally

1 Talking about yourself

You will learn

- to exchange greetings
- to ask Greeks simple questions about themselves
- to answer simple questions about yourself
- to understand a Greek customs official
- to recognize some common Greek names and forms of address

Before you begin

Try to listen to the first three dialogues with your book handy but *closed*. You will hear people greeting one another. Then rewind and listen again to each dialogue separately studying the notes. Follow the same pattern with the remaining dialogues. Don't worry, you will not understand every word on the tape at first, but you should concentrate on the gist and the rhythm of the language. When you are satisfied that you understand the dialogues, move on to the *Key words and phrases* and then follow the pattern set out in the *Study guide* below. You may find it useful to tick off each stage as you complete it. The presenter will guide you through each unit and refer you back to the *Study guide* when necessary.

Study guide

	Dialogues 1–3: listen without the book
	Dialogues 1–3: listen, read and study one by one
	Dialogues 4–6: listen without the book
	Dialogues 4–6: listen, read and study one by one
	Dialogues 7, 8: listen without the book
	Dialogues 7, 8: listen, read and study one by one
	Study *Key words and phrases*
	Complete the exercises in *Practice what you have learned*
	Study *Grammar* and do the exercises
	Do *The Greek alphabet*
	Read *Did you know?*
	Do the taped exercises in *Your turn to speak*
	Finally, listen to all the dialogues again

Dialogues

1 *Sofia arrives at a hotel she has stayed at before*

Sofia Kalimera sas kírie Niko.
Niko Kalimera sas.

Kírios

Kiria

Despinís

2 *Eli and Kanela don't know each other very well*

Eli Kalimera. Ti kánete?
Kanela Kalá, ke esís?
Eli Polí kalá.

♦ **kalá** fine, well, all right
♦ **ke** and
♦ **polí** very

3 *Eleni meets a friend's son in the park*

Eleni Kalimera.
Yiannis Kalimera sas.
Eleni Ti kanis?
Yiannis Kalá, esís?
Eleni Kalá, efharistó.

♦ **efharistó** thanks

1 ♦ **kalimera sas** good morning (lit. good day to you). This is the way to greet someone you don't know well or a number of people.
♦ **kírie** Mr/sir. To be polite, you should use **kírie** when you are addressing a man and **kiria** when you are addressing a woman. **Kírie** is often followed by the man's first name (e.g. **kírie Niko**). Equally **kiria** (Mrs) is followed by the first name (e.g. **kiria Eleni**). The Greek word for 'Miss' is **despinís**, so you can say **despinís Sofia** (Miss Sophie).

Two other greetings you should know are:
♦ **kalispera** good afternoon (after siesta), good evening
♦ **kalinihta** good night

Note Don't forget to pay particular attention to the stress on words where it is marked.

2 ♦ **ti kánete?** how are you? (how do you do?)

esís you. There are two ways of saying 'you' in Greek: a polite form for people you don't know well or when you're talking to more than one person and a form you use with friends and children. **Esís**, you, and **sas**, (to) you, are both polite forms.

3 ♦ **ti kanis?** how are you?/how do you do? **Kánete** (in dialogue 2) and **kanis** both mean literally 'you do'. You should use **kánete** when you speak to someone you don't know well or to more than one person and **kanis** when you speak to a child or a friend. Note also that in Greek there is no need to use the English 'you', the idea is contained in the ending of the verb: **kan-is**, **kán-ete**.

4 *You bump into someone in a store – oh sorry!*

Anna Ah. . .! Signomi.
Nina Den pirazi, den pirazi, endaksi.

5 *Getting through the Greek customs*

Teloniakós Signomi, apó pou ísaste?
ipálilos
Tourístria Ime apó tin Anglia.
Teloniakós Milate katholou elliniká?
ipálilos
Tourístria Ne, milao ligo, alá katalaveno.
Teloniakós Polí orea. Doste mou sas parakaló to diavatirió sas.
ipálilos
Tourístria Efharistos. Oriste.

teloniakós ipálilos customs officer
tourístria tourist (woman)
♦ **ne** yes (**ohi** no)
♦ **alá** but
♦ **orea** good, fine

4 ♦ **signomi** sorry, also means 'excuse me'. You can use it to begin a conversation (see dialogue 5).

♦ **den pirazi** it doesn't matter. **Den** in front of the verb makes the sentence negative. The negative will be explained in more detail on p. 45.

♦ **endaksi** it's all right/OK.

5 ♦ **signomi** excuse me. A very useful word to begin a conversation.

♦ **apó pou ísaste?** where are you from? (lit. from where are you?)

♦ **ime apó tin Anglia** I'm from England. **Anglia** is used in Greek to mean both England and Britain.

♦ **milate (katholou) elliniká?** do you speak Greek (at all)? You'll probably want to ask: **milate angliká?** do you speak English? In order to ask a question in Greek use a questioning tone of voice. **Milate elliniká** said as a flat statement means 'you speak Greek'.

milao ligo I speak a little. Note again that you don't need a separate word for I (**egó**) and you (**esís**): **milao** (I speak), **milate** (you speak).

♦ **katalaveno** I understand.

doste mou . . . to diavatirió sas give me . . . your passport (lit. the passport your).

♦ **sas parakaló** please (lit. you I ask/request). The officer is being formal. 'Please' is normally just **parakaló**.

♦ **efharistos** gladly, with pleasure. Don't confuse this word with **efharistó** (thank you).

♦ **oriste** This is a word you will hear a lot in Greece. It has different meanings, but in this case it means 'here it is'.

6 *Two tourists meet on the beach. They both turn out to be English.*

Kírios	Kalimera kiria.
Kiria	Kalimera kírie.
Kírios	Ti kánete?
Kiria	Kalá, esís?
Kírios	Etsi ki etsi. Ime kourasmenos. Iste Anglida?
Kiria	Ne, ime. Ke esís?
Kírios	Ke egó ime Anglos. Ti kánete stin Ellada?
Kiria	Kano tis diakopés mou.

egó I

egó   **esís**

7 *Two women meet and ask each other's names*

Vivi	Pos sas lene?
Vasiliki	Me lene Vasiliki. Esás, pos sas lene?
Vivi	Vivi.

8 *Kírios Diamantis meets a little girl. What's her name?*

Kírios D.	Pos se lene?
Vaso	Vaso.
Kírios D.	Vaso? Ah! oreo ónoma.

oreo beautiful, pretty
to ónoma name.

6   **etsi ki etsi** so so.

ime kourasmenos I'm tired. If a woman were speaking she would say: **ime kourasmeni**. **Kourasmenos** is an adjective and has to agree with the person (masculine or feminine) it is describing. To take another example: If you want to know if 'he' is married, it's **iste pandremenos?** (**pandremeni** if you are asking a woman). More on adjectives can be found on p. 101.

◆ **iste** (short for **ísaste**) **Anglida?** are you English? (i.e. an Englishwoman). However, changing the intonation would turn the phrase into the statement 'you are English'. The use of **Anglida** shows that he is talking to a woman. So **Anglida** is a feminine noun. Some other feminine forms of nationalities are: **Ellinida** (a Greek woman), **Italida** (an Italian woman) and **Gallida** (a French woman).

◆ **ime Anglos** I'm English (i.e. an Englishman). **Anglos** is a masculine noun. Here are some other masculine forms of nationalities: **Gallos** (a Frenchman), **Yermanós** (a German man) and **Italós** (an Italian man). However, a Greek man is **Éllinas**.

ti kánete stin Ellada? what are you doing in Greece? Do you remember: **ti kánete?** (how are you?/how do you do?) in dialogue 2? Here you have the basic meaning of the verb **kano** (I do).

◆ **kano tis diakopés mou** I'm on vacation (lit. I'm doing the vacations my). Note that **mou** (my), **sas** (your) etc. come *after* the noun - **diakopés mou** (my vacation(s)).

7 ◆ **pos sas lene?** what's your name? (lit. how do they call you?). This is the formal way of asking an adult his or her name. The familiar form is **pos se lene?**

◆ **me lene Vasiliki** my name's Vasiliki (lit. me they call Vasiliki).

esás you. This is the emphatic form and means the same as **esís**.

8   **pos se lene?** what's your name? (lit. how do you they call?) This is how you might ask the name of a child or an adult in an informal atmosphere. The reply would be just the name by itself or **me lene**. . .

Key words and phrases

These are the words and phrases introduced in the dialogues which you will need to know how to say.

To learn

kalimera	good morning
kalispera	good afternoon/evening
efharistó	thank you
parakaló	please
signomi	sorry, excuse me
den pirazi	it doesn't matter
oriste	here you are
ke	and
alá	but
polí	very
ne	yes
ohi	no
endaksi	all right, OK
orea	good, fine
ime Anglos/Anglida	I'm English
milate elliniká?	do you speak Greek?
milao ligo	I speak a little
ti kánete stin Ellada?	what are you doing in Greece?
kano tis diakopés mou	I'm on vacation
pos sas/se lene?	what's your name?
me lene. . .	my name is. . .

To understand

ti kánete?	how are you?
kalá, ke esís?	fine, and you?
ime kourasmenos/kourasmeni	I'm tired
apó pou ísaste?	where do you come from?
iste (ísaste) Éllinas/Ellinida?	are you Greek?

Practice what you have learned

This part of the unit is to help you to recognize the language in the dialogues with more confidence. You will need both the book and the cassette to do the exercises which follow, but detailed instructions for each exercise will be in your book. The language to be practiced involves using greetings, introducing yourself and asking and answering simple questions. You will have a chance to speak later in the unit.

1 Listen to the tape where you will hear four short dialogues. (You may want to listen to them a couple of times.) Tick the correct answer to the question on each dialogue below. (Answers p. 20)

1 The man is **a.** ☑ asking the girl's name.

b. ☐ asking her how she is.

2 Yiorgo is feeling **a.** ☐ tired.

b. ☑ fine.

3 The man is **a.** ☐ German.

b. ☑ English.

4 Yiorgo and Maria exchanging greetings **a.** ☐ in the evening.

b. ☑ at night.

2 Listen to the tape. The presenter will give you four clues in English. Think of the Greek word to use and write it in the spaces below. Then down the shaded line in the puzzle you will find the Greek word for 'fine, well'. (Answers p. 20)

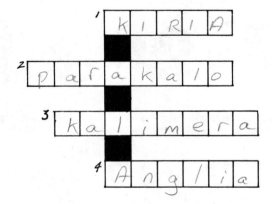

1. K I R I A
2. p a r a k a l o
3. k a l i m e r a
4. A n g l i a

3 Listen to the tape and fill in the missing words in the dialogue.

Kírios _Kalimera_ ....

Kiria Kalimera, ti _kanete_ .... ?

Kírios Kalá, _efharisto_ ..... ke ..... _esis_ .... ?

Kiria ..... _etsi_ ..... ki _etsi_ ....., ime _kourasmeni_ .....

Kírios ..... _ti_ ..... kánete stin _Ellada_ .... ?

Kiria Káno tis ..... _diakoupes_ .... mou.

esís	etsi	diakopés		Ellada	kourasmeni
kalimera	etsi		kánete	efharistó	ti

4 Listen to the tape. A Greek man is asking a girl some questions. The pictures below illustrate the girl's answers. Put a check next to the picture you think illustrates the correct answer. (Answers p. 20)

1a ☑   2a ☐   3a ☐   4a ☑

1b ☐   2b ☑   3b ☑   4b ☐

5 For this exercise do exactly as for exercise 4. Listen to the tape again. This time a Greek woman is asking a man some questions. (Answers p. 20)

1a ☑   2a ☑   3a ☑

1b ☐   2b ☐   3b

Grammar

Verbs

You have met two important verbs in this unit. First let's look at the present tense of the verb **kano** (to do).

kano	I do, I am doing	**kánoume**	we do, we are doing
kanis	you do, you are doing	**kánete**	you do, you are doing
kani	he/she/it does he/she/it is doing	**kánoune**	they do, they are doing

Note the following points:

1 The endings of Greek verbs change to show the person or persons involved. So there's no need to use the pronouns I, you, he etc. except for emphasis.
2 In Greek the present tense translates both the English 'I do' and 'I am doing'.
3 In Greek there are two ways of saying 'you . . .' do something. You use **kanis** (you do) for a child or one person you know well (the familiar form) and **kánete** (you do) for one person you don't know well (the polite form) or when you're talking to more than one person.
4 **Kano** has the same pattern of endings as many other common Greek verbs.

Ime

Start by learning the important, but irregular verb 'to be'. (Note, however, that there is no infinitive in Greek; the basic form of the verb is the 'I' form. So the verb 'to be' in Greek is literally the verb 'I am', the verb 'to do' is the verb 'I do' and so on.)

ime	I am	**ímaste**	we are
ise	you are	**ísaste (iste)**	you are
ine	he/she/it is	**ine**	they are

Iste is simply a shortened form of **ísaste**. As you can see, the singular 'he/she/it is' and the plural 'they are' are both **ine**.

Exercise 1 Translate the following into Greek. (Answers p. 20)
a. We are **b.** you do (familiar form) **c.** they are **d.** I am doing **e.** he does **f.** she is **g.** I am **h.** you are doing (polite form) **i.** we do **j.** it is **k.** you are (polite form).

Exercise 2 The verbs in the following sentences are incomplete. You should add the missing letters. (Answers p. 20)

a.	.... m ..e..... stin Ellada	I am in Greece
b.	i..ma....s...t..e polí kalá	We are fine
c.	..ísa.s...t.e.. pandremenos?	Are you married?
d.	...i.me..... kalá	I am fine
e.	ís..a.s.te......e kourasmenos	You are tired
f.	i..me...... pandremeni	I am married
g.	in **c** above a woman is being addressed true/false
h.	in **f** above a woman is speaking true/false

The Greek alphabet

As you probably know, Greeks do not use the Latin alphabet as we do, although with the growth of tourism to Greece it is becoming more and more common to find signs, menus etc. in Greek with an accompanying transliteration into the Latin alphabet.

In the introduction, we explained why we will not be teaching the whole Greek alphabet until Unit 13. However, strange alphabets can be fun – rather like codes – and so that you can have a taste of the Greek script, in this section we will introduce two letters of the Greek alphabet in each unit. We will start in this unit with *alfa* and *kapa*.

Letter	Name	Equivalent sound in English
A α	alfa	'a' as in father
K κ	kapa	'k' as in key

First cover the left-hand column and underline the new letters. Then uncover it and read the words out loud.

kalimera	καλημέρα
kalispera	καλησπέρα
Anglia	'Αγγλία
kalá	καλά
kourasmenos	κουρασμένος
katalaveno	καταλαβαίνω
kírios	κύριος
kiria	κυρία
Anglida	'Αγγλίδα
kano	κάνω

Did you know?

Greece is made up of a jagged peninsula and over 2,000 islands. It has a population of about 9.5 million, well over a third of whom live in the Athens-Piraeus area. The landscape is dominated by two elements – mountains and the sea. About 80 per cent of the land is mountainous and no part of the country is more than 100 kilometers from the sea. Some of the largest mountains like Olympus and Taiyetos are only a few kilometers from the coast.

Greece enjoys a classic Mediterranean climate; a short spring is followed by a long hot summer and an extended autumn. The winter is short but can be very cold, particularly in the mountains and in the north. Regular snowfalls on higher ground make skiing possible. In summer one needs only light clothes, especially in the cities where it can be very hot and dusty; however, it can get chilly at night by the sea and on the islands. On average there are 3,000 hours of sunshine a year.

Greek products

Despite the difficult conditions for agriculture Greece produces good quality fruits (peaches, oranges, water and honey melons) and vegetables (tomatoes, eggplants, zucchini, etc). Greek olives, olive oil and honey are very fine and a good value to buy instead of more traditional souvenirs. You can buy local food products at the open market (**agorá**) in most towns and at the itinerant popular markets (**laikí agorá**) which are set up on different days in different neighborhoods in the larger towns. If you want to buy local wines look out for small wineshops with large wooden barrels. You can either bring your own bottles to fill up or pay a returnable deposit on a jug (**galoni**). Most wineshops will have a choice of draught wines and you're always welcome to try a glass before deciding which one to buy.

Modern Greece

In 1453 Constantinople, the capital of the Byzantine Empire, fell to the Ottoman Turks. By this time most of the Greek mainland and some of the islands were already in Ottoman hands. There followed nearly four hundred years of Turkish rule. During the late eighteenth century a feeling of Greek national self-consciousness began to emerge, particularly among expatriate Greeks. Within Greece itself resistance to the Turks existed but was sporadic and disorganized. However a full-scale armed revolt broke out in the Peloponnese in 1821 and the fighting spread to other parts of the country. The Greek cause won wide support in Europe and many Philhellenes ('lovers of Greece') went to fight in Greece, including Lord Byron. As the war continued a number of European governments took a more active role and even intervened directly. Finally, British, French and Russian ships destroyed an Egyptian fleet sent by the Sultan to regain control of the Peloponnese at Navarino Bay in 1827. This action assured victory for the Greeks and the foundation of an independent state.

The new state consisted of the Peloponnese, part of Thessaly and some of the islands. After some searching a ruler approved by the Powers was found in 1832 and a Bavarian prince became King Otho I of Greece. Otho ruled until 1862 when he was overthrown and replaced by a Danish prince who became King George I. This second king ruled for nearly fifty years during which time Greece expanded her territory to roughly the borders it now occupies.

Greece fought on the side of the Allies in World War I. Following the collapse of the Ottoman Empire, Greece occupied western Asia Minor but was defeated by the Turks in 1922. Greece and Turkey subsequently agreed to an exchange of populations on a religious basis and some 1.5 million Greek refugees came to Greece.

Greece fought again with the Allies in World War II. After the liberation of the country from the Germans in 1944 the communist party tried to seize power. There followed a disastrous civil war which ended with the defeat of the communists in 1949.

Even during peacetime the Greek political scene has tended to be volatile. The system of government itself has changed several times in the present century and the state has been at some times a monarchy and at others a republic. Following the fall of the military junta which ruled for seven years until 1974, Greece became once again a democratic state and, following a referendum, a republic. The country became a full member of the EEC in 1982.

Your turn to speak

In these exercises you will be taking part in a conversation or exchange. Alexandros will tell you what to say, in English. After his prompt, stop the tape, work out what to say and then say it loud and clear in Greek. Then start the tape again and you will hear the correct sentence. You might find this type of exercise a bit complicated at first, but try it once or twice and you'll soon get used to it.

1 You will practice **kalimera**, **kalispera** and asking and answering simple questions.

2 Here you will have a short conversation, this time about where you come from, what you're doing in Greece and about how well you speak Greek.

Answers

Practice what you have learned p. 15 Exercise 1 1a, 2b, 3b, 4b.

p. 15 Exercise 2 kiria, parakaló, kalimera, Anglia = KALA

p. 16 Exercise 4 1a, 2b, 3b, 4a.

p. 16 Exercise 5 1a, 2a, 3a.

Grammar p. 17 Exercise 1 (a) ímaste (b) kanis (c) ine (d) kano
(e) kani (f) ine (g) ime (h) kánete (i) kánoume (j) ine (k) ísaste/iste.

p. 17 Exercise 2 (a) ime (b) ímaste (c) ise (d) ime (e) ísaste/iste
(f) ime (g) false (h) true.

2 Yourself and others

You will learn

- to ask and answer questions about the family
- to talk about jobs
- to understand and reply to simple introductions
- the numbers up to 20

Before you begin

Listen to the first three dialogues without using the book. You will learn some more questions to ask people and what to reply when you are introduced. Then listen to these dialogues again looking at the text and studying the notes. Continue to work through the unit following the study pattern set out in the *Study guide* below. You will be following the same general pattern throughout the course, so you should soon be familiar with the method of working.

Study guide

	Dialogues 1–3: listen without the book
	Dialogues 1–3: listen, read and study one by one
	Dialogues 4, 5: listen without the book
	Dialogues 4, 5: listen, read and study one by one
	Dialogues 6–8: listen without the book
	Dialogues 6–8: listen, read and study one by one
	Study *Key words and phrases*
	Complete the exercises in *Practice what you have learned*
	Study *Grammar* and do the exercises
	Do *The Greek alphabet*
	Read *Did you know?*
	Do the taped exercises in *Your turn to speak*
	Finally, listen to all the dialogues again

Dialogues

1 *Sofia meets a child in her hotel. Where was he born? How old is he?*

Sofia	Pos se lene?
Jimi	Jimi.
Sofia	Pou yeníthikes?
Jimi	Stin Amerikí.
Sofia	Se pió meros?
Jimi	Sti Nea Yiorki.
Sofia	Poso hronón ise?
Jimi	Deka ke misó.

deka ten
misó half

2 *Pleased to meet you*

Anna	Pió ine to onomá sas kírie?
Yiorgos	Yiorgos Tolios.
Anna	Hero polí.
Yiorgos	Hero polí.

1 **pou yeníthikes?** where were you born? **Pou** is the word for 'where' e.g. **pou ine i Kavala?** where is Kavala?

stin Amerikí in America.

se pió meros? in which place?

♦ **poso hronón íse?** how old are you? **Poso** means 'how much/many' and **hronón** is the word for 'time' or 'age'.

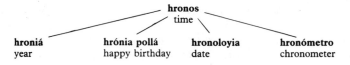

	hronos time		
hroniá year	**hrónia pollá** happy birthday	**hronoloyia** date	**hronómetro** chronometer

2 ♦ **pió ine to onomá sas kírie?** what is your name, sir? This is an alternative to **pos sas lene** which you learned in Unit 1.

to onomá sas your name (lit. the name yours). In Greek all nouns are divided into three types or *genders*: masculine, feminine and neuter. You can often tell which gender a noun is from its ending – masculine nouns in the singular end in **-os**, **-is** or **-as**; feminine nouns in **-i** or **-a** and neuter nouns in **-i**, **-o**, or **-ma**. If the word has 'the' in front of it you can tell which gender it is immediately: **o kírios** (Mr/sir) is masculine, **i kiria** (Mrs/ the woman) is feminine and **to ónoma** (the name) is neuter. The word for 'the' is used much more in Greek than in English e.g. **i Anglia** England. (You will find more examples in Unit 4.)

In some cases, in words of more than two syllables whose stress is not on the last syllable, the stress is moved to the last syllable before possessive pronouns (in this case **sas**) for easier pronunciation.

♦ **hero polí** pleased to meet you (lit. I am pleased very). You should say this when you are introduced or repeat it if someone says it to you first.

3 *Katerina meets a very elegant young lady. What's her job?*

Katerina Kalimera pos se lene?
Eleni Me lene Eleni.
Katerina Ke ti douliá kanis?
Eleni Ime aerosinodós.

4 *Anna meets a nice young man at the bar; but she is not alone . . .*

Anna Ti douliá kanis?
Lakis Ime mihanikós. Esí ti douliá kanis?
Anna Ime grammatévs.
Lakis Ise pandremeni?
Anna Ne, ime. Aftós ine o andras mou.
Lakis Ah! Hero polí.

> **o mihanikós** mechanic, engineer
> **i grammatévs** secretary

5 *Maria introduces her sister Vivi to Viky*

Viky Kalispera, ti kánete?
Maria Kalá efharistó, k'esís?
Viky Polí kalá.
Maria Apo'dó i adelfí mou.
Viky Oh! hero polí.
Vivi Episis.
Viky Apó pou ísaste?
Vivi Apó tin Walia.
Viky Apó pió meros akrivós?
Vivi Apó to Swansea.

i Walia Wales

3 ♦ **ti douliá kanis?** what work do you do? **I douliá** and **i aerosinodós** are feminine nouns.

♦ **ime aerosinodós** I'm an air hostess. Note that you leave out the 'a' or 'an' when you state your profession, so **ime mihanikós** (I'm an engineer), **ime grammatévs** (I'm a secretary).

4 ♦ **ise pandremeni?** are you married? Remember if you were asking a man you would say **ise pandremenos?**

aftós ine o andras mou this is my husband. **Aftós** (this) changes according to whether the noun is masculine, feminine or neuter e.g. **aftós ine o stathmós** (this is the station), **aftí ine i yineka mou** (this is my wife), and **aftó ine to onomá sas** (this is your name).

yineka

yinekologos   **yinekologia**
gynaecologist   gynaecology

5 **k'esís?** and you? (short form of **ke esís**).

apo'dó i adelfí mou over here (is) my sister (lit. from here . . .). **Apo'dó** (over here) is the short form of **apó edó**.

♦ **episis** also, too. If someone says **hero polí** you can either say **hero polí** in reply or **episis** – (pleased to meet you) too, (me) too.

apó pió meros akrivós? from which place exactly?

6 *Vivi introduces Viky to her mother*

Vivi   Na sas sistiso ti mitera mou.
Viky   Oh! hero polí.
Maria   Episis.
Viky   Apó pou ísaste?
Maria   Apó tin Anglia.
Viky   Ah! eho mia adelfí stin Anglia sto Brighton, ehi dio kores ke ena yió.

7 *Yiorgos is asking Vivi some questions about herself*

Yiorgos   Apó pou ine o andras sas?
Vivi   Ine Amerikanós.
Yiorgos   Éhete pediá?
Vivi   Ne, eho dio pediá.
Yiorgos   Ti douliá kánete?
Vivi   Ime daskala.

8 *A child is counting*

Pedí   Ena (1), dio (2), tria (3), téssera (4), pende (5), eksi (6), eftá (7), októ (8), enea (9), deka (10), éndeka (11), dódeka (12), dekatria (13), dekatéssera (14), dekapende (15), dekaeksi (16), dekaeftá (17), dekaoktó (18), dekaenea (19), íkosi (20).

6 ♦ **na sas sistiso ti mitera mou** may I introduce my mother to you.

eho mia adelfí stin Anglia I have a sister in England. The other parts of **eho** (I have) are listed in *Grammar*. Note that the word for 'a' or 'an' changes according to the gender of the noun: **enas mihanikós** (a mechanic) is masculine, **mia adelfí** (a sister) is feminine and **ena diavatírio** (a passport) is neuter.

ehi dio kores ke ena ýió she has two daughters and a son.

7 **apó pou ine o andras sas?** where is your husband from? (lit. from where is . . .?).

♦ **éhete pediá?** do you have children? **To pedí** (child).

ime daskala I'm (a) teacher. **I daskala** (teacher).

pedagogía	pedíatros	pedikós stathmós	pedaki
education	pediatrician	nursery	little child

8 ♦ **ena, dio, tria** one, two three . . . Learn these numbers by heart.

Key words and phrases

To learn

hero polí	pleased to meet you
epísis	me too, also, likewise
ime aerosinodós	I'm (an) air hostess
ime grammatévs	I'm (a) secretary
ime kathiyitís	I'm (a) professor
ime mihanikós	I'm (an) engineer
eho dio pediá	I have two children
ena	one
dio	two
tria	three
téssera	four
pende	five
eksi	six
eftá	seven
októ	eight
enea	nine
deka	ten
éndeka	eleven
dódeka	twelve
dekatria	thirteen
dekatéssera	fourteen
dekapende	fifteen
dekaeksi	sixteen
dekaeftá	seventeen
dekaoktó	eighteen
dekaenea	nineteen
íkosi	twenty

To understand

pió ine to onomá sas?	what's your name?
poso hronón iste/ise?	how old are you?
ti douliá kánete/kanis?	what work do you do?
pou doulévete?	where do you work?
ise pandremenos/pandremeni?	are you married?
éhete pediá?	do you have children?
na sas sistiso	may I introduce you to. . .?

Practice what you have learned

This part of the unit is to help you to recognize the language in the dialogues with more confidence. You will need both the book and the cassette to do the exercises which follow. You will practice understanding family relationships, other people's jobs and numbers.

1 Complete the following conversation. The questions are in your briefcase. When you have filled in the gaps check with the tape for the correct version.

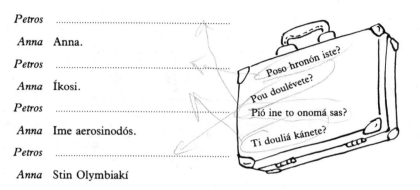

Petros ....

Anna Anna.

Petros ....

Anna Íkosi.

Petros ....

Anna Ime aerosinodós.

Petros ....

Anna Stin Olymbiakí

In the briefcase:

Poso hronón iste?

Pou doulévete?

Pió ine to onomá sas?

Ti douliá kánete?

2 First listen to the tape. You will hear six people telling you their names and their jobs. Fill in the correct job in the boxes below. The jumbled words will help you. (Answers on p. 34)

grammatévs

mihanikós

aerosinodós

ipálilos

kathiyitís

daskala

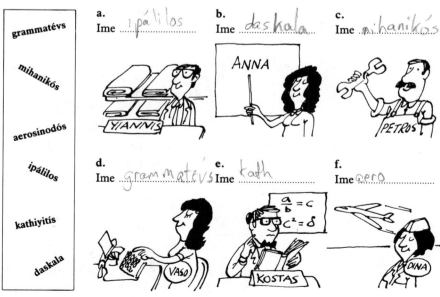

a. Ime *ipálilos*

b. Ime *daskala*

c. Ime *mihanikós*

d. Ime *grammatévs*

e. Ime *kath*

f. Ime *aero*

3 You'll need to know your numbers up to 20 before trying this one. Here is your bingo card. Listen to the tape, the caller will say all the numbers except one. You should cross out those he says. What are you left with?

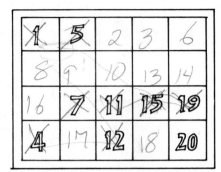

4 There is only one correct version of each of these sentences. Make your own choice and then check with the tape to see if you're right.

1 Aftós ine o ....a. ☒ andras mou
                                        b. ☐ adelfí mou
                                        c. ☐ pedí mou

....

2 Aftí ine i ....a. ☐ adelfós mou
                                        b. ☒ mitera mou
                                        c. ☐ andras mou

....

3 Aftós ine o ....a. ☐ kori mou
                                        b. ☒ pateras mou
                                        c. ☐ adelfí mou

....

4 Aftí ine i ....a. ☐ andras mou
                                        b. ☐ pateras mou
                                        c. ☒ kori mou

....

When you have checked your answers with the tape write the translation of the correct sentence in the space provided. (Answers p. 34)

Grammar

Eho and doulevo

The next most important verb after 'I am' (**ime**) is the verb 'I have' (**eho**).
Here is the present tense.

eho I have   **éhoume** we have
ehis you have   **éhete** you have
ehi he/she/it has   **éhoune** they have

Remember Greek verbs do not have to have pronouns (I, you, we, etc.).
Pronouns are only used for emphasis, e.g. **egó eho** (*I* have). There is
another common verb in this unit: **doulevo** (to work). Note the endings are
the same as **eho** and **kano** in Unit 1.

doulevo I work/I'm working
doulevis you work/you are working
doulevi he/she/it works/he/she/it is working

doulévoume we work/we are working
doulévete you work/you are working
doulévoune they work/they are working

Exercise 1   Parts of the verb **eho** are missing from the following sentences. Can you complete them?. (Answers p. 34)

a. E ..*hete*..... pediá?   Do you have any children?

b. ...*Eho*.... o mia adelfí stin Anglia   I have a sister in England.

c. E. *h*.i dio kores   She has two daughters.

d. ......*Eh*.....ou.....*ne*....... polá leftá   They have a lot of

money.

Exercise 2   Write the verb **piano** (I take/catch) in full.
Piano has the same endings as **kano, eho, doulevo**. (Answer p. 34)

piano

.....*piano*......
.....*pianis*......
.....*piani*......
.....*pianoume*......
.....*pianete*......
.....*pianoune*......

The Greek alphabet

Letters you have already met

A	α	'a' as in father
K	κ	'k' as in key

New letters

Letter	Name	Equivalent sound in English
E ε	épsilon	'e' as in let
Δ δ	delta	In between 'd' and 'th' but 'd' as in door is acceptable

First cover the left-hand column and underline the new letters. Then uncover it and read the words out loud.

diavatírio	διαβατήριο
Eleni	Ἐλένη
Ellada	Ἑλλάδα
dio	δύο
doulevo	δουλεύω
aerosinodós	ἀεροσυνοδός
egó	ἐγώ
eho	ἔχω
kalimera	καλημέρα
aerodrómio	ἀεροδρόμιο

Did you know?

Traveling to Greece

British, Canadian, American and Common Market citizens need only a passport to enter Greece for periods of up to three months. If you arrive by boat or by air you will be asked to complete an immigration card.

When entering Greece by car (be warned it's a hazardous and tiring trip especially through Yugoslavia) you need to take
- your car registration or an International Registration Certificate available from national automobile organizations
- a 'Green Card', international comprehensive insurance
- your driver's license.

You should also make sure that you are insured against illness and accidents. The Greek public health service is extremely limited.

And what is your name?

Pos se lene?

In most Greek families first names are handed down in a set pattern. A man names his first son after his own father and sometimes adds his own name to distinguish him from his cousins. Look at this typical family tree.

Kanela = Panayiotis Marcopoulos

Alexandros = Sofia   Nikos = Anna   Maria = Dimitris

Panayiotis (Alexandros) 1960   Panayiotis (Nikos) 1964   Panayiotis (Dimitris) 1968

Greek people do not name their children until the baptism and they then use the names of saints in the Greek calendar. This is very important as they do not celebrate their birthday but their 'name day'. It's much easier for friends to remember the name day, even shops display the days for the most popular names and Greeks receive lots of telegrams and telephone calls on their day wishing them and their family **hrónia pollá** – 'many years'. Here are some of the most common names and their dates.

George **Yiorgos** April 23	John **Yiannis** August 6
Constantine **Constandinos** May 21	Spyro **Spyridon** December 12
Helen **Eleni** May 21	Mary **Maria** or **Despina** August 15
Nicholas **Nikos** December 6	

Some parents give their children classical Greek names, e.g. Evrodiki (Eurydice), Achilleas (Achilles) and Ektoras (Hector). However, these names are always followed by a saint's name.

Your turn to speak

Read the instructions to the exercises and then work with the tape alone. Alexandros will tell you what to do. You will have to answer questions about your family and work and then ask similar questions yourself. You will also practice numbers.

1 In this exercise you will be practicing, **hero polí, epísis** and **ti douliá kánete?**

2 You will be practicing numbers:

1	5	7	10	12
10	15	20	17	4

Answers

Practice what you have learned p. 29 Exercise 2 (a) ime ipálilos (b) ime daskala (c) ime mihanikós (d) ime grammatévs (e) ime kathiyitís (f) ime aerosinodós.

p. 30 Exercise 4 1 (a) This is my husband   2 (b) This is my mother 3 (b) This is my father   4 (c) This is my daughter.

Grammar p. 31 Exercise (1) (a) éhete (b) eho (c) ehi (d) éhoune.

p. 31 Exercise 2 piano, pianis, piani, piánoume, piánete, piánoume.

3 Ordering drinks and snacks

You will learn

- to ask if something is free
- to order coffee, tea, wine etc.
- to order your breakfast
- to understand vocabulary for certain Greek specialties
- to ask what things are and give your order
- the numbers 20 – 50

Before you begin

Listen to the dialogues paying particular attention to the main vocabulary used to order drinks and snacks. Try to pick out words you have already met. Practice the most important phrases (listed for you on p. 42). As usual we advise you to follow the study pattern set out below and tick off each part of the unit in the box provided as you complete it.

Study guide

	Dialogues 1–4: listen without the book
	Dialogues 1–4: listen, read and study one by one
	Dialogues 5–9: listen without the book
	Dialogues 5–9: listen, read and study one by one
	Study *Key words and phrases*
	Complete the exercises in *Practice what you have learned*
	Study *Grammar* and do the exercise
	Do *The Greek alphabet* and complete the exercise
	Read *Did you know?*
	Do the taped exercises in *Your turn to speak*
	Listen to all the dialogues again
	Finally, do *Revision/Review Units 1–3* at the end of the book

Dialogues

1 *You are hot and tired. Is this chair free?*

Eleni   Signomi, ine eléftheri aftí i karekla?
Maria   Ne.
Eleni   Efharistó.
Maria   Parakaló.

♦ **i karekla** chair

2 *Maria would like to order some coffee but not Greek coffee*

Maria   Thelo ena nescafé.
Servitora   Me gala?
Maria   Ohi, sketo.
Servitora   Oriste.
Maria   Efharistó.

♦ **me** with
♦ **to gala** milk
  i servitora waitress

3 *Eleni wants to try a Greek coffee and cheese pies*

Eleni   Ti ine aftó?
Pedí   Ine ellinikós kafés.
Eleni   Mou férnete ena, parakaló.
Pedí   Amesos.
Eleni   Ke . . . dio tirópites.
Pedí   Ah! tirópites den éhoume, spanakópites mono.
Eleni   Ah! Kalá, den pirazi.

1 ♦ **ine eléftheri aftí i karekla?** is this chair free? (lit. is it free this chair?). Because **i karekla** is feminine the other words **eléftheri** (free) and **aftí** (this) have the feminine ending for adjectives **-i** to agree with the noun. You will be given more details on the gender of nouns in the grammar section of Unit 4.

♦ **parakaló** not at all (lit. please). This is the polite reply when someone says 'thank you'. It is said very frequently and is also used if someone says **signomi** (sorry!) to mean 'not at all, that's alright!'

2 ♦ **thelo** I would like (lit. I want). Here are some other examples of how the ending of the verb indicates 'I' e.g. **eho, doulevo, kano.**

ena nescafé a coffee, not necessarily a *Nescafé*, any instant coffee, but not Greek coffee.

sketo plain (in this case, black coffee). Most coffee is served with sugar (**me záhari**) and without milk, but in summer you might want to ask for iced-coffee **frapé: thelo ena frapé** (I want an iced coffee) or if you want more than one **thelo dio frapé** (I want two iced coffees).

♦ **oriste** This is an all purpose word, you find it meaning 'what would you like?', 'yes', and even 'what are you doing here?' Here it means 'here it is'.

3 ♦ **ti ine aftó?** what's this? It's not always easy to find a written menu in Greece so you may have to point to what you want.

ellinikós kafés Greek coffee. It is very strong, and made of fine-ground coffee heated with water and sugar in a small pot (**briki**). It is served in small cups with a glass of water.

♦ **mou férnete ena** bring me one (Greek coffee). Remember you learned **enas** (a, an, one with masculine words) e.g. **enas andras** (a man), **mia** (a, an, one, with feminine words) e.g. **mia tirópita** (a cheese pie), and **ena** with neuter words e.g. **ena yiaourti** (a yoghurt). **Férnete** (you bring), **ferno** (**I bring**).

♦ **amesos** immediately.

♦ **den éhoume** we don't have any (lit. we don't have). In Greek it is not necessary to use a specific word for 'any'; it is understood.

spanakópites mono spinach pies only.

4 *Eleni's being inquisitive again – what's this? It looks like milk but it turns out to be stronger*

Eleni	Ti ine aftó?
Servitora	Ine ouzo, me neró.
Eleni	Poso ine?
Servitora	Ine íkosi drahmés.
Eleni	Efharistó.
Servitora	Parakaló.

♦ **to neró** water
drahmés drachmas

5 *Maria and Vivi are ordering breakfast*

Garsón	Kalimera kiries.
Maria	Kalimera.
Vivi	Kalimera.
Garsón	Ti thelete yiá proinó?
Maria	Thelo tsai me lemoni.
Vivi	Egó thelo ena nescafé me gala.
Maria	Éhete fresko psomí?
Garsón	Ohi, distihós den ehoume.
Maria	Ti krima! Ferte mas dio friganiés, voútiro, marmelada.
Vivi	Egó thelo ke dio avgá vrastá.
Garsón	Amesos.

6 *Kírios Manolis, the baker, is serving Vaso*

Vaso	Yiá sas kírie Manoli. . .
Kírios Manolis	Yiá sou koritsi mou.
Vaso	. . . éhete tirópites?
Kírios Manolis	Pos, orees, poli orees.
Vaso	Kotópites, spanakópites?
Kírios Manolis	Ne ne, ola, apola apola.
Vaso	Thelo n'mou dósete mia kotópita, mia spanakópita . . .
Kírios Manolis	Málista.
Vaso	. . . ke mia tirópita.
Kírios. Manolis	Orea. Dódeka ke tris: dekapende, íkosi ke trianda: peninda. Efharistó.

kotópites chicken pies
♦ **málista** yes, certainly

4   **ouzo me neró** ouzo with water. Ouzo is a very popular drink in Greece. It is an anise-flavored spirit and a refreshing aperitif when served with ice and water. Although clear and colorless, it goes a cloudy white when water is added.

♦ **poso ine?** how much is it? This is a common and easy way of asking the price. It is very simple to use because if you want to know the price of one or more than one thing you say the same **poso ine?** Remember that **ine** means 'he/she/it is' or 'they are' (see again p. 17).

5 ♦ **ti thelete yiá proinó?** what would you like for breakfast?

♦ **thelo tsai me lemoni** I'd like tea with lemon.

♦ **egó thelo ena nescafé me gala** I'd like a coffee with milk. Here the addition of the **egó** before the verb is for emphasis and means 'as for me. . .'

♦ **éhete fresko psomí?** have you got fresh bread?

♦ **ohi, distihós den ehoume** no, unfortunately we don't (lit. we don't have).

♦ **ti krima!** what a pity!

ferte mas dio friganiés, voútiro, marmelada bring us two toasts, butter and jam. Note that **friganiés** are continental-style toasts (hard, crisp bread) in bags which are served instead of toast. **Tost** in Greek is a toasted sandwich. Also, **marmelada** means any kind of jam.

♦ **egó thelo ke dio avgá vrastá** I'd like two boiled eggs, too. The word for boiled (**vrastá**) follows the word for eggs (**avgá**); fried eggs are **avgá tiganitá**. Here the word **ke** does not mean 'and' but 'too/as well' e.g. **k'egó** (me too).

6 ♦ **yiá sas** hello/goodbye (lit. health to you). This is the polite form, or for when you're talking to more than one person. The familiar form is **yiá sou**; kírios Manolis says **yiá sou** because Vaso is a child.

koritsi mou my girl. The addition of **mou** makes the greeting more friendly. Other examples: **despinís mou, kiria mou.**

♦ **pos, orees, poli orees** of course, good, very good (ones).

ne ne, ola, apola apola yes yes, all, all kinds, all kinds.

thelo n'mou dósete I want you to give (to) me. You should say **thelo na mou dósete** (Vaso has blurred the **na** and **mou** because she is speaking quickly). **Na** is used to link two verbs e.g. **thelo na eho** I want to have.

dódeka ke tris: dekapende twelve and three: fifteen.

íkosi ke trianda: peninda twenty and thirty: fifty.

7 *Maria and Anna are tired after their shopping and stop for a snack*

Anna	Maria, ti tha párete?
Maria	Egó, mia koka kola, ke dio tirópites; esís ti tha párete?
Anna	Egó tha paro mia tirópita ke ligo krasaki.
Maria	Lipón.
Anna	Garsón, sas parakaló, ferte, mia tirópita, ena krasaki. . .
Maria	Mia koka kola ke ales dio tirópites.
Garsón	Amesos, tha ta fero.
Anna	Efharistoume polí.
Garsón	Parakaló.
Anna	Garsón, parakaló.
Garsón	Ti thélete?
Anna	To logariasmó mas.
Garsón	Ne, amesos.

8 *Children on the beach rush to the ice-cream stall*

Servitora	Edó, ta kalá pagotá, elate korítsia.
Nina	Yiá sas, thelo ena honaki me lemoni, fraoula ke kakao.
Servitora	Ke esí despinís?
Vaso	Egó thelo ena kipelaki me fráoula – eh – vanilla ke vísino.
Servitora	Endaksi.

to honaki cone, cornet
ta fráoula strawberries
to kakao cocoa
to kipelaki little tub
to vísino sour cherry

9 *The numbers twenty to fifty*

íkosi ena (21), íkosi dio (22), íkosi tria (23), íkosi téssera (24),
íkosi pende (25), íkosi eksi (26), íkosi eftá (27), íkosi októ (28),
íkosi enea (29), trianda (30), saranda (40), peninda (50).

7 ◆ **ti tha párete?** what would you like? (lit. what will you take?). The **tha** in front of the verb makes it future. Note the use of the polite form of the verb (**párete**); the familiar form would be **paris**.

egó tha paró *I'll* have (lit. *I'll* take). The use of the pronoun **egó** is only for emphasis.

ke ligo krasaki and a little wine. The word for wine is **krasí**, but in this case, the speaker has made it diminutive by adding the ending **-aki** which is used to make things smaller e.g. **pedí** (child), **pedaki** (little child). As Anna says **ligo** (a little) as well, she means: 'and just a drop of wine'. However, the Greeks use diminutives very freely and the **-aki** often denotes sentimental familiarity or endearment rather than size.

◆ **lipón** so, well then, let's see. This is a very common and useful word – it can give you time to think e.g. **lipon . . . thelo** (well then/let's see I'd like . . .).

ales dio tirópites another two cheese pies. The word for 'another' has to change to agree with the noun: **alos kafés** (another coffee) is masculine, **ali tirópita** (another cheese pie) is feminine, **alo krasi** (another wine) is neuter. The plurals are: **ali** (masculine), **ales** (feminine) and **ala** (neuter).

◆ **amesos, tha ta fero** at once, I'll bring them.

efharistoume polí we thank you very much.

◆ **to logariasmó mas** our bill (lit. the bill our). You could say simply **to logariasmó** (the bill).

8 **edó, ta kalá pagotá** here, the good ice creams. **Ta pagotá** is the plural of **to pagotó** (ice cream).

elate (korítsia) come on (girls).

◆ **endaksi** all right, OK.

9 ◆ **íkosi ena . . .** As before learn these numbers by heart.

Key words and phrases

To learn

ti ine aftó?	what's this?
lipón	so, well then, let's see
thelo ena kafé	I'd like a coffee
ena nescafé	an instant coffee
ena frapé	an iced coffee
me gala	with milk
thelo voútiro	I'd like some butter
marmelada	some jam
thelo krasí	I'd like wine
koka kola	coke
thelo mia tirópita	I'd like a cheese pie
mia spanakópita	a spinach pie
thelo dio tirópites	I'd like two cheese pies
tris koka koles	three cokes
éhete psomí?	do you have any bread?
éhete friganiés?	do you have any (continental) toast?
mou férnete neró	would you bring me some water
mou férnete ena tsai me lemoni	would you bring me a tea and lemon
ti krima!	what a pity!
to logariasmó	the bill
poso ine?	how much is it?
yiá sas	good-bye
endaksi	all right, OK

íkosi ena	21	trianda	30
íkosi dio	22	trianda dio	32
íkosi tria	23	trianda pende	35
íkosi téssera	24	saranda	40
íkosi pende	25	saranda ena	41
íkosi eksi	26	saranda dio	42
íkosi eftá	27	saranda októ	48
íkosi októ	28	saranda enea	49
íkosi enea	29	peninda	50

To understand

ti tha párete?	what would you like?
ti thélete yiá proinó?	what would you like for breakfast?
oriste	here you are
distihós den eho	unfortunately I don't have
den éhoume	we don't have
parakaló	please, not at all
orea	good, fine
amesos	immediately
málista	yes, certainly
pos	certainly, of course

Practice what you have learned

This part of the unit is to help you to recognize the language in the dialogues with more confidence. You will need both the book and the cassette to do the exercises which follow. Here you will be asked to understand the language used to order snacks and drinks.

1 Look carefully at the drawing and tick the phrase you would use to reply. Check with the tape to see if your answers are correct.

☑ Kalimera kírie   ☐ Ena krasaki, parakaló
☐ Kalimera kiria   ☑ Ena frapé, parakaló

2 Complete the following conversation with the help of the tape and the drawing.

Garsón   Ti thélete yia ...*proinó*...............?

Maria   Thelo ena ...*nescafe*........... me ...*gala*...............

Garsón   Ke esís?

Yiorgos   Thelo ena ...*tsai*............... me ...*lemoni*...............

Garsón   Amesos.

Maria   Thelo ...*voútiro*..........., ...*Marmelada*..., ke
...*friganies*....

Yiorgos   Thelo dio ...*avga*...................

3 Listen to the tape and tick the correct answer to each question.
(Answers p. 48)

1 ti thélete?

a. ☐ ena kipelaki me fráoula ke kakao
b. ☑ ena kipelaki me fráoula ke lemoni
c. ☐ ena honaki me fráoula ke lemoni

poso ine?

d. ☐ deka drahmés
e. ☑ íkosi drahmés
f. ☐ deka pende drahmés

2 ti thélete?

a. ☑ ena ouzo me neró
b. ☐ ena kafé me gala
c. ☐ ena frapé me gala

poso ine?

d. ☐ ikosi drahmés
e. ☐ peninda drahmés
f. ☑ deka pende drahmés

4 Here you have a list of things. Listen to the tape and tick the boxes
according to whether the café has them or not. (Answers p. 48)

	Yes	No
tirópites	☐	☑
spanakópites	☑	☐
nescafé	☐	☑
tsai	☑	☐
koka kola	☐	☑
krasí	☑	☐

5 Listen to the tape and write down the prices of each item as in the example.
(Answers p. 48)

Ellinikós kafés ....*30*.......Δρχ

Nescafé ....*20*.......Δρχ

me gala ....*25*.......Δρχ

Tsai ....*15*.......Δρχ

me lemoni ....*20*.......Δρχ

Voútiro ....*35*.......Δρχ

Marmelada ....*29*.......Δρχ

Psomí ....*5*.......Δρχ

Avgá ....*30*.......Δρχ

Grammar

Asking questions

You have seen that you can change a statement into a question by using a questioning tone of voice: **milate (katholou) elliniká?** do you speak Greek (at all)? (Unit 1, dialogue 5), **ine eléftheri aftí i karekla?** is this chair free? (Unit 3, dialogue 1), **me gala?** with milk? (Unit 3, dialogue 2). You have also seen questions formed by using question words.

ti? what?   **ti douliá kanis?** what work do you do?

pos? how?   **pos sas lene?** how do they call you? (i.e. what's your name?)

piós? who? (masculine)   **piós ine?** who is he?

piá? who? (feminine)   **piá ine?** who is she?

pió? what, which (neuter)   **pió ine to onomá sas?** what is your name?

poso? how much?   **poso ine?** how much is it/are they?

Make sure you know these important question words and learn the examples to help you remember them.

The negative

To make a sentence negative you put **de(n)** in front of the verb.

thelo kafé I want coffee   **de thelo kafé** I don't want coffee
milao elliniká I speak Greek   **de milao elliniká** I don't speak Greek

Before vowels and a few consonants (k, p, t, b, ks, and ps) **de** becomes **den** to make it easier to say with the word that follows.

éhoume we have   **den éhoume** we don't have
ime Ellinida I'm a Greek   **den ime Ellinida** I'm not a Greek (woman)

Exercise Make the following sentences negative by using **de(n)** and then translate them into English. (Answers p. 48)

a. ......*De*..... thelo gala   *want Milk*

b. Aftí i karekla ......*den*..... ine eléftheri   *not Free*

c. ......*den*...... ehoume psomí   *have bread*

d. ......*Den*...... ine Amerikanós   *not Am*

e. ......*De*...... milao angliká   *Speak Eng.*

Thelo

Here is the present tense of another useful verb **thelo** (I want)

thelo   I want   **théloume**   we want
thelis   you want   **thélete**   you want
theli   he/she/it wants   **théloune**   they want

Note that **thelo** is not as abrupt as the English 'I want'; it can often be used where we would use 'would like' in English. So, **thelo** I want/I'd like, **ti thélete?** what do you want/would you like?

The Greek alphabet

Letters you have already met

A	α	'a' as in father
Δ	δ	'd' as in door
E	ε	'e' as in let
K	κ	'k' as in key

New letters

Letter	Name	Equivalent sound in English
M μ	mi	'm' as in my
Φ φ	fi	'f' as in four

First cover the left-hand column and underline the new letters. Then uncover it and read the words out loud.

kafés	καφές
frapé	φραπέ
farmakio	φαρμακείο
fresko	φρέσκο
me	μέ
mera	μέρα
fráoula	φράουλα
friganiá	φρυγανιά
marmelada	μαρμελάδα
fotografia	φωτογραφία

Here is part of the menu of a continental breakfast.

Exercise

ΚΟΝΤΙΝΕΝΤΑΛ

ΤΣΑΪ	ΚΑΦΕΣ		ΓΑΛΑ	☐
μὲ ΓΑΛΑ ☐	ΓΑΛΛΙΚΟΣ	☐ ΣΟΚΟΛΑΤΑ		☐
μὲ ΛΕΜΟΝΙ ☑	ΑΜΕΡΙΚΑΝΙΚΟΣ		☑ ΒΟΥΤΥΡΟ	☐
ΦΡΥΓΑΝΙΕΣ ☐	ΝΕΣΚΑΦΕ		☑ ΜΑΡΜΕΛΑΔΑ	☐
ΨΩΜΙ ☑	ΕΛΛΗΝΙΚΟΣ		☐ ΜΕΛΙ	☐

Now look at the same menu transcribed from the Greek letters. Eleni wants tea with lemon, bread, butter and marmalade. Which boxes should she tick to place her order? (Answers p. 48)

KONTINENTAL

TSAI	KAFES	
☐ me GALA	☐ GALLIKOS	☐ GALA
☐ me LEMONI	☐ AMERIKANIKOS	☐ VOUTIRO
☐ FRIGANIES	☐ NESCAFE	☐ MARMELADA
☐ PSOMI	☐ ELLINIKOS	☐ MELI

Did you know?

Breakfast and snacks

Most Greeks eat a very light breakfast usually consisting of a cup of coffee or a glass of hot milk and a piece of bread with jam or honey. It is common to have a snack in the middle of the morning. In the towns people buy toasted sandwiches (**tost**) or hot pies from small shops and stalls. Pies are made of puff or phyllo pastry with different fillings e.g. **tirópita** (feta cheese pie), **spanakópita** (spinach pie) and **kotópita** (chicken pie). In the country people eat bread with a few olives and some **feta** (soft white cheese made from sheep's milk). Lunch (**yevma**) is eaten late – normally between two and three o'clock and is traditionally followed by a siesta.

If you are invited to a Greek house you will most likely be given a cup of Greek coffee, a glass of cold water and something sweet. The sweet is sometimes a spoonful of jam or almond paste (especially in the country) or a cake such as **katayifi** (shredded wheat with nuts and honey) or **baklavá** (layers of phyllo pastry with nuts and honey). As sugar is added to the coffee while it is being heated you will be asked how you like it: **sketo** (plain, no sugar), **métrio** (medium) or **glykó** (sweet).

Here is how to make Greek coffee:

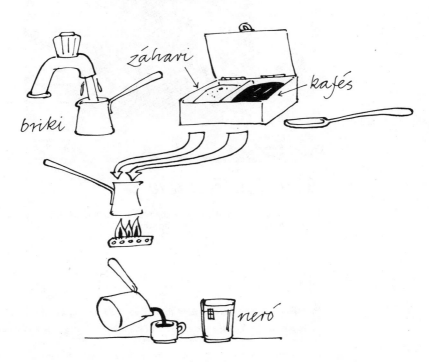

Other Greek sweets you may like to try:

bougatsa flaky pastry filled with custard
halvás cakes made of nuts, semolina, sugar and cinnamon or crushed sesame seeds
loukoumathes small doughnuts deep fried in oil and served with honey

Your turn to speak

Read the instructions to the exercises and then work with the tape alone, paying particular attention to the intonation and pronunciation of the phrases to be practiced. The Greeks enjoy little snacks at all times of the day. You are going to order in a small café.

1 Before going to eat in the **taverna** you decide on an aperitif. You will practise **thelo** (I'd like) and **poso ine?** (how much?).

2 It's midday and everyone around you is eating pies. You'd like to try them. You will practice ordering 'one' of something and understanding the cost – **peninda drahmés**, and more numbers.

Revision/Review

Now turn to p. 213 and complete the revision section on Units 1–3. On the cassette *Revision* follows straight after this unit.

Answers

Practice what you have learned p. 44 Exercise **3** 1b, 1e; 2a, 2f.

p. 44 Exercise **4 Yes** spanakópites, tsai, krasí **No** tirópites, nescafé, koka kola.

p. 44 Exercise **5** nescafé 20, nescafé me gala 25, tsai 15, tsai me lemoni 20, voútiro 35, marmelada 27, psomí 5, avgá 30.

Grammar p. 45 (a) **de** I don't want milk (b) **den** this chair is not free (c) **den** we don't have bread (d) **den** he isn't American (e) **de** I don't speak English.

The Greek alphabet p. 46 tsai me lemoni, psomí, voútiro and marmelada.

4 Getting information

You will learn

- to ask and understand where something is situated
- how to change money at the bank
- the numbers 50–100
- to explain that you don't understand
- how to book rooms at a hotel

Do you remember?

I'd like a little wine	thelo krasaki
have you any bread?	éhete psomí?
how much is it?	poso ine?
10	deka
11	éndeka
20	íkosi

Before you begin

By now you should be familiar with the pattern of study. Follow the instructions set out in the *Study guide* below and mark off each section as you complete it.

Study guide

	Dialogues 1–4: listen without the book
	Dialogues 1–4: listen, read and study one by one
	Dialogues 5, 6: listen without the book
	Dialogues 5, 6: listen, read and study one by one
	Dialogues 7, 8: listen without the book
	Dialogues 7, 8: listen, read and study one by one
	Study *Key words and phrases*
	Complete the exercises in *Practice what you have learned*
	Study *Grammar*
	Do *The Greek alphabet* and complete the exercise
	Read *Did you know?*
	Do the taped exercises in *Your turn to speak*
	Finally, listen to all the dialogues again

Dialogues

| | **1** | *It's disco time, but where's the discotheque?* |

Eleni Parakaló, pou ine i diskoték?
Pedí   Ine sto ipóyio.
Eleni Efharistó.

| | **2** | *It is a very hot day, where is the bar?* |

Sofia   Parakaló, pou ine to bar?
Yiorgos Ine sto proto órofo.
Sofia   Efharistó.
Yiorgos Parakaló.

to bar bar

| | **3** | *The hotel manager's son is counting and a guest interrupts him to ask where to change a travellers' cheque* |

Pedí   Íkosi (20), trianda (30), saranda (40), peninda (50), eksinda (60), evdominda (70), ogdonda (80), eneninda (90), ekató (100).
Kiria Parakaló, pou boró n'alakso ena travellers chek?
Pedí   Oriste, na to grafio edó pera.
Kiria Pió sigá. Ti ípate? Den katálava.

1 ♦ **pou ine i diskoték?** where is the disco? You learned in Unit 1 that **ine** means 'is' or 'are', now you can use **pou ine?** in the singular or in the plural e.g. **pou ine o stathmós?** (where is the station?), **pou ine i toualetes?** (where are the toilets?).

sto ipóyio in the basement.

ipóyio

2 ♦ **ine sto proto órofo** it's on the first floor. The picture shows the words for the basement, the ground floor and the floors above.

trito órofo

déftero órofo

proto órofo

isóyio

ipóyio

3 ♦ **pou boró n'alakso?** where can I change? As you learned in Unit 3, to link two verbs you use the word **na** (here the **na** has been run into the following word). For example: **pou boró na pao?** where can I go? (**pao** I go), **boró na eho?** can I have? **thelo na pao** I want to go.

oriste, na to grafio here you are! here's the office. This **na** means simply 'here!' or 'there!' 'There it is!' is **na to!**

♦ **edó (pera)** (over) here. '(Over) there' is **ekí (pera)**. Both **edó** (here) and **ekí** (there) can be used on their own.

♦ **pió sigá. Ti ípate? Den katálava** more slowly. What did you say? I didn't understand.

UNIT 4

4 *At the bank kiria Anna wants to change some dollars*

Kiria Anna — Sas parakaló kírie, pou boró n'alakso dollária?
Kírios — Ne, edó sto proto tamio.
Kiria Anna — Efharistó polí.
Kírios — Parakaló.

to dollário dollar
ta dollária dollars

5 *Katerina wants to change some sterling travellers' cheques*

Katerina — Tha íthela n' alakso aftá ta travellers cheks.
Tamias — Málista, apó piá hora ine parakaló?
Katerina — Apó Anglia.
Tamias — Apó Anglia? To diavatirió sas tha'thela.
Katerina — Ne, oriste, poso ine tora i lira edó stin Ellada?
Tamias — Símera, nomizo ine ekatón dio drahmés ke trianda.
Katerina — Endaksi.
Tamias — Ipográpsete edó parakaló.
Katerina — Oriste, endaksi.
Tamias — Peráste sto tamio me ta travellers chek ke tin apódiksi yiá na paralávete ta hrimatá sas.
Katerina — Efharistó.
Tamias — Yiá sas.
Katerina — Andío sas.

o tamias cashier
i lira pound sterling

6 *Sofia asks a question but Anna's reply is so fast that she doesn't understand*

Sofia — Parakaló, pou boró n'alakso lires?
Anna — Edó sto ksenodohio despinís alázoun, alá an thélete borite na pate apénandi pou ine i trápeza.
Sofia — Ti ípate? Den katálava, pió sigá parakaló.
Anna — Sto ksenodohio alazoune lires, alá an thélete edó apénandi ine ke i trápeza.

4 ne, edó sto proto tamio yes, here at the first teller's window.

5 ♦ tha íthela I would like. This is another form of thelo. We have seen that thelo is not as abrupt as the English 'I want'; however, tha íthela (or the shortened form tha'thela) is the polite form of thelo, so it's worth remembering as an alternative.

♦ málista, apó piá hora ine parakaló? yes (certainly), from which country are they please?

ne, oriste, poso ine tora i lira edó stin Ellada? yes, here you are, how much is the pound now in Greece? (lit. how much is it now the pound. . .).

símera, nomizo ine ekatón dio drahmes ke trianda today, I think it is 102 drachmas and 30 (lepta). Nomizo (I think) has the same endings as kano, thelo etc. 100 lepta = 1 drahma.

♦ ipográpsete edó sign here.

♦ peraste sto tamio go to the teller's window (lit. pass to the teller's window).

me ta travellers chek ke tin apódiksi with the travellers' cheques and the receipt. I apódiksi, but after me (with), i becomes ti(n) e.g. me ti yineka (with the woman), me tin karekla (with the chair). Ti becomes tin before vowels and certain consonants to make it easier to say.

yiá na paralávete ta hrimatá sas in order to collect your money. Another word for hrímata (money) is leftá.

♦ andio sas good-bye (to you). You could simply say andio.

6 edó sto ksenodohio, despinís, alazoun here is the hotel, Miss, they change (them). Alazo (I change) has the same endings as thelo (I want) and kano (I do).

♦ alá an thélete but if you want. To say 'if' simply put an in front of the verb e.g. an borite (if you can).

borite na pate apénandi you can go across the street. Note again the use of na to link two verbs. Pate (you go) from pao (I go).

pou ine i trapeza where there is the bank.

♦ ti ípate? Den katálava, pió sigá parakaló what did you say? I didn't understand, more slowly please.

edó apénandi ine ke i trapeza (lit.) here across the street there's the bank too.

7 Booking a room in a small hotel

Kiria Anna   Hérete kírie.

Ksenodohos   Hérete.

Kiria Anna   Éhete eléfthera domátia?

Ksenodohos   Ena leptó parakaló. Ti thélete monó i dipló?

Kiria Anna   Dipló.

Ksenodohos   Ena leptó . . . ne, eho. Yiá poses meres?

Kiria Anna   Yiá tris meres sas parakaló.

Ksenodohos   Endaksi, to diavatirió sas, sas parakaló.

Kiria Anna   Oriste kírie.

Ksenodohos   Efharistó.

Kiria Anna   Sas parakaló, poso ine tin iméra?

Ksenodohos   Pendakóses drahmés.

Kiria Anna   Me proinó?

Ksenodohos   Me proinó.

o ksenodohos hotelier
pendakoses 500

8 Booking for yourself and your children

Ksendohos   Kalimera sas.

Kiria   Eléfthera domátia éhete?

Ksenodohos   Eksartate, ti domátia thélete?

Kiria   Tha íthela ena – er – dio domátia, to ena me dipló krevvati ke to alo me dio moná.

Ksenodohos   Dio leptá parakaló. Veveos, éhoume.

Kiria   To thelo apó tin proti eos tis deka pende Avgoustou.

Ksenodohos   Proti eos deka pende Avgoustou? Nomizo ine eléfthera, den éhoume kanena próvlima.

Kiria   Efharistó.

Ksenodohos   Yiá sas, ke sas éfhoume kalí paramoní stin patrída mas.

Kiria   Efharistó.

7 ♦ **éhete eléfthera domátia?** do you have (any) free rooms? Do you remember **aftí i karekla ine eléftheri** is this chair free? Here the word **eléfthera** agrees with **domátia** (rooms) the plural of the neuter **to domátio** (the room). You'll find more about adjectives on p. 101.

ena leptó one minute, moment.

♦ **monó i dipló** single or double (room)?

kírie sir. **O kírios** becomes **kírie** when you are speaking directly to a man. This happens only with masculine nouns.

♦ **me proinó** with breakfast. Here are some other useful phrases: **me dous** (with shower), **me bánio** (with bathroom), **me balkoni** (with balcony).

♦ **yiá poses meres?** for how many days? You may also need to understand: **yiá poses nihtes?** (for how many nights?), **yiá posa átoma?** (for how many people?).

♦ **poso ine tin imera?** how much is it per day? 'A week/per week' is **tin evdomada**.

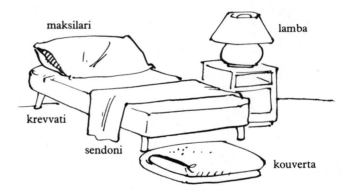

maksilari
lamba
krevvati
sendoni
kouverta

8 **eksartate** it depends.

♦ **to ena me dipló krevvati** one with a double bed (lit. the one with double bed).

♦ **ke to alo me dio moná** and the other with two singles.

♦ **veveos** certainly.

♦ **to thelo** I want it. Here the **to** refers to the neuter noun **domátio** (room); if it referred to a feminine noun like **karekla** (chair) it would be **ti thelo**.

♦ **apó tin proti eos tis dekapende Avgoustou** from August 1 to 15. Here **Avgoustos** (August) changes its ending to **Avgoustou** to mean 'of August'. Note also that after **apó** (from), as after **me** (with), **i** becomes **ti(n)** e.g. **apó tin Anglia** (from England); **apó ti yineka** (from the woman).

kanena provlima no problem at all.

sas efhoume kalí paramoní we wish you a pleasant stay.

stin patrida mas in our country. **Stin** is made by combining **se** (in/to) and **ti(n)** (the). So **se** + **tin Athina** becomes **stin Athina** (in/to Athens), **se** + **to Londino** becomes **sto Londino** (in/to London).

Key words and phrases

To learn

pou ine?	where is/are?
pou boró n'alakso. . .	where can I change. . .
travellers cheks?	travellers' cheques?
lires?	pounds?
dollária?	dollars?
edó	here
ti ípate?	what did you say?
den katálava	I didn't understand
pió sigá	more slowly
éhete eléfthera domátia?	do you have free rooms?
thelo ena monó domátio	I'd like a single room
ena dipló domátio	a double room
me proinó	with breakfast
me bánio	with a bathroom
me dous	with shower
me balkoni	with a balcony
me ena dipló krevvati	with a double bed
me dio moná krevvátia	with two single beds
poso ine tin imera?	how much is it a day?
andio	good-bye

eksinda	60	evdominda	70
eksinda ena	61	evdominda ena	71
eksinda dio	62	ogdonda	80
eksinda tria	63	ogdonda ena	81
eksinda téssera	64	eneninda	90
eksinda pende	65	eneninda ena	91
eksinda eksi	66	eneninda enea	99
eksinda eftá	67	ekató	100
eksinda októ	68		
eksinda enea	69		

To understand

ine sto. . .	it's on the. . .
isóyio	ground floor
proto órofo	first floor
déftero órofo	second floor
trito órofo	third floor
ine sto ipóyio	it's in the basement
apénandi	in front of/across the street
apó piá hora ine?	from which country is it?
ipográpsete	sign
peraste sto tamio	go to the teller's window
yiá poses meres?	for how many days?
nihtes?	nights?
yiá posa átoma?	for how many people?
veveos	certainly
an thélete	if you want/like

Practice what you have learned

In the following exercises you will be asked to recognize the phrases used for booking rooms, changing money and asking questions. Read the instructions to each exercise before switching on the tape.

1 You and your wife want a room for five nights. Listen to the tape and complete your part of the conversation. (Answers p. 62)

a. ...... *Kalimera* ......

b. ...... *Fhete eleftera domátia* ......

c. ...... *jia dio* ......

d. ...... *jia pende meves* ......

e. ...... *Oriste* ......

f. ...... *efharistó* ......

2 Where are all these places? Listen to the tape and tick the correct answer. (Answers p. 62)

1 Parakaló, pou ine i diskoték?
- **a.** ☐ sto proto órofo
- **b.** ☐ sto trito órofo
- **c.** ☑ sto ipóyio

2 Parakaló, pou ine to bar?
- **a.** ☐ sto proto órofo
- **b.** ☐ sto ipóyio
- **c.** ☑ sto deftero órofo

3 Parakaló, pou ine to domatió mou?
- **a.** ☑ sto trito órofo
- **b.** ☐ sto ipóyio
- **c.** ☐ sto déftero orofo

3 Listen to the tape where you will hear a man changing money and place a tick by the correct picture. (Answer p. 62)

4 Listen to the tape and complete the dialogue with the correct numbers. (Answers p. 62)

Tamias Kalimera sas, ti thélete parakaló?

Kiria Thelo na alakso .....*10*............. lires. (£10, £5, £60, £15)

Tamias Amesos.

Kiria Poso ine i lira símera edó stin Ellada?

Tamias .....*115*............. drahmés. (100 drs, 120 drs, 75 drs, 115 drs)

Kiria Endaksi, ke aftá ta travellers cheks, parakaló.

Tamias Apó piá hora ine?

Kiria Apó tin Anglia.

Tamias Posa ine?

Kiria .....*100*............. lires. (£200, £60, £50, £100)

5 Select the Greek phrase which corresponds to the English in 1, 2 and 3. Check with the tape afterwards.

1 What did you say?
a. ☐ pou ine?
b. ☑ ti ípate?
c. ☐ apó piá hora ine?

2 I didn't understand
a. ☐ den eho
b. ☑ den katálava
c. ☐ de milao

3 More slowly please
a. ☐ signomi
b. ☐ posa ine
c. ☑ pió sigá, parakaló

Grammar

Nouns

As we have seen, all nouns in Greek are masculine, feminine or neuter. You can usually tell which gender a noun is by its ending: masculine nouns in the singular end in **-os**, **-is** or **-as**; feminine nouns in **-i** or **-a** and neuter nouns in **-i**, **-o** or **-ma**. However, if the word has 'the' in front of it we can tell which gender it is immediately:

o andras (man) is masculine
i yineka (woman) is feminine
to diavatírio (passport) is neuter.

Similarly, the different forms of 'a', 'an' or 'one' indicate the gender of the word that follows:

enas tamias (a/one cashier) is masculine
mia trápeza (a/one bank) is feminine
ena domátio (a/one room) is neuter.

You will have noticed that 'the' (**o**, **i** or **to**) is used much more frequently than in English:

o andras mou ine mihanikós my husband is a mechanic
aftí i karekla ine eléftheri this chair is free
pió ine to onomá sas? what is your name?

You should also note that proper names and place names belong to one of the three genders and often have 'the' in front of them e.g. **o Petros** (Peter), **i Maria** (Mary), **i Athina** (Athens), **to Londino** (London).

Accusative Case

When the noun is the _object_ of the sentence or when it follows words like **apó** (from), **me** (with) and **se** (to/in):

o becomes **to(n)**
i becomes **ti(n)**
to remains **to**
However, don't worry about this – when it does happen it will be pointed out and explained.

If you want to say 'some' or 'any' simply leave out 'a/the' e.g.

to psomí (the) bread   **psomí** some/any bread
to krasí (the) wine   **krasí** some/any wine

The verb to note in this unit is **boró** (I can)

boró	I can	**boroume**	we can
borís	you can	**borite**	you can
borí	he/she/it can	**boroune**	they can

Remember how to put two verbs together with **na**:

boró na pao   I can go
boroume na pároume we can take

The Greek alphabet

Letters you have already met

A α	'a' as in father
Δ δ	'd' as in door
E ε	'e' as in let
K κ	'k' as in key
M μ	'm' as in my
Φ φ	'f' as in four

New Letters

Letter	Name	Equivalent sound in English
I ι	yiota	'i' as in police
T τ	taf	't' as in tip

First cover the left-hand column and underline the new letters. Then uncover it and read the words out loud.

tamias	ταμίας
tsai	τσαί
trápeza	τράπεζα
trapezi	τραπέζι
Italia	Ἰταλία
honaki	χονάκι
krevvati	κρεββάτι
apénandi	ἀπέναντι
psomí	ψωμί
ti	τί

Exercise You need to change money. Tick the place you have to go to. (Answers p. 62)

1 a. ☑ TRAPEZA ΤΡΑΠΕΖΑ   b. ☐ KSENODOHIO ΞΕΝΟΔΟΧΕΙΟ

2 Which of these two words means 'breakfast'?
   a. ☐ PROTO ΠΡΩΤΟ   b. ☑ PROINO ΠΡΩΙΝΟ

3 You are in the bank. Where is the teller's window?
   a. ☑ TAMIO ΤΑΜΙΟ   b. ☐ TOUALETA ΤΟΥΑΛΕΤΑ

4 Which is the word for room?
   a. ☑ DOMATIO ΔΩΜΑΤΙΟ   b. ☐ KREVVATI ΚΡΕΒΒΑΤΙ

Did you know?

Where to stay

Greek hotels are classified in six categories: AA or de luxe and A to E (1st to 5th class). There are also a number of government Xenia hotels which vary in category but are all comfortable. The lower category hotels are clean and adequate and some of them occupy charming old buildings. In all hotels the price of the room should be displayed on a card on the back of the door. You should check if breakfast is included in the price of the room. When you arrive, the hotel may keep your passport for the first night.

It is possible to rent rooms in private houses in most places; local tourist offices and the tourist police keep lists of recommended rooms and control the prices. Apartments and villas where you can do your own cooking are also available.

Campsites operated by the NTOG, the Hellenic Touring Club and the Greek Automobile and Touring Club can be found in most popular resorts. It is advisable to use official sites and not to camp in the open. Prices are very reasonable and there is a 10% reduction if you have a camping booklet. There are also a few youth hostels and, in Athens, a YMCA and YWCA for holders of international YMCA and YWCA cards. More information on all kinds of accommodations can be obtained from the Greek National Tourist Office, Olympic Tower, 645 5th Ave., New York, NY 10022.

Changing money

Travellers' cheques and currency can be changed at border entry points, ports and airports at all times and in many shops. You will need your passport when changing checks. Banks are open from 8:00 a.m.–1 p.m. (Monday–Saturday) and in tourist centers some banks are open in the afternoon. The National Bank of Greece in Sintagma Square in Athens is open until 8:00 p.m. In villages where there are no banks, the main banks have agents – usually local shopkeepers – who can change money. You may find you have a long wait to change money in smaller banks – particularly on the islands.

Your turn to speak

Read the instructions to the exercises and then work with the tape alone.
You will have to take part in two conversations. Alexandros will tell you
what to say.

1 You are going to practice booking rooms at a hotel – **éhete eléfhera
domátia, thelo, monó/dipló**.

2 You are at the bank, **trápeza**. You will practice changing money **thelo na
alakso travellers cheks, den katálava, pió sigá**, and some more numbers.

Answers

Practice what you have learned p. 57 Exercise 1 (a) kalimera (b) éhete
eléfthera domátia? (c) yiá dio (d) yiá pende meres (e) oriste
(f) efharistó.

p. 57 Exercise 2 1c, 2c, 3a.

p. 58 Exercise 3 You should have ticked the second picture.

p. 58 Exercise 4 £10, 115 drs, £100.

The Greek alphabet p. 59 1a, 2b, 3a, 4a.

5 Directions

You will learn

- to ask for directions to the bank, the tourist office and the bus
- to understand where places are situated
- to understand simple directions
- to ask for information to be repeated
- numbers 100–500

Do you remember?

I want to change travellers' cheques	**thelo na alakso travellers cheks**
I want a double room	**thelo ena dipló domátio**
it's on the second floor	**ine sto déftero órofo**
52	**peninda dio**
65	**eksinda pende**
70	**evdominda**
100	**ekató**
83	**ogdonda tria**
97	**eneninda eftá**

Before you begin

Work through this unit very carefully, you will often have to ask for and understand directions. As usual mark off the sections in the *Study guide* below as you complete them.

Study guide

	Dialogues 1–6: listen without the book
	Dialogues 1–6: listen, read and study one by one
	Dialogues 7–10: listen without the book
	Dialogues 7–10: listen, read and study one by one
	Dialogues 11, 12: listen without the book
	Dialogues 11, 12: listen, read and study one by one
	Study *Key words and phrases*
	Complete the exercises in *Practice what you have learned*
	Study *Grammar* and do the exercises
	Do *The Greek alphabet* and complete the exercise
	Read *Did you know?*
	Do the taped exercises in *Your turn to speak*
	Finally, listen to all the dialogues again

Dialogues

1 *A child asks where the post office is*

Pedí   Parakaló, pou ine to tahidromio?
Kiria To tahidromio ine diakosa metra deksiá.
Pedí   Efharistó.

to tahidromio post office

2 *In a taverna, kiria Anna wants to know where the toilet is*

Kiria Anna   Parakaló, pou ine i toualeta?
Ipálilos   Ne, sto vathos aristerá.
Kiria Anna   Efharistó.
Ipálilos   Parakaló.

3 *A woman asks the hotel receptionist if there is a bank nearby*

Kiria   Kírie sas parakaló, iparhi mia trápeza edó kondá?
Kírios Ne, edó apénandi.
Kiria   Ah! Efharistó polí.

4 *Eleni has a headache so she's looking for a pharmacy*

Eleni Parakaló, pou iparhi ena farmakio?
Maria Trito stenó, aristerá.
Eleni Efharistó.
Maria Parakaló.

5 *Now, where's the tourist office?*

Eleni Parakaló, pou ine to touristikó grafio?
Maria Tha pate ísia brostá ke tha to dite.
Eleni Efharistó.
Maria Parakaló.

to touristikó grafio tourist office

ísia brostá

aristerá   deksiá

1 ◆ **diakosa metra deksiá** 200 meters on the right. Remember in Greece you have to use meters and kilometers. Here are more examples, **ine ekató metra deksiá** (it is a hundred meters on the right), **ine ena hiliómetro deksiá** (it is one kilometer on the right), **ine trakosa metra deksiá** (it is three hundred meters on the right).

2 ◆ **sto vathos aristerá** in the back on the left. Here is another example with **aristerá: ine ekató metra aristerá** (it is 100 meters on the left).

3 ◆ **iparhi mia trápeza?** is there a bank? **Iparhi** means 'there is/exists'. Also remember to change the 'a' or 'an' according to the gender of the noun: for example, **enas stathmós** (a station) is masculine, **mia trápeza** (a bank) is feminine and **ena tahidromio** (a post office) is neuter.

◆ **edó kondá** near here (lit. here near).

4 **pou iparhi ena farmakio?** where is a pharmacy?

◆ **trito stenó aristerá** third street on the left. **Ena stenó** is a side street or lane; the adjective **stenós, -i, -o** means narrow e.g. **ena stenó domátio** a narrow room. 'Road' is **o dromos**.

5 ◆ **tha pate (ísia brostá)** you should go (straight ahead) (lit. you will go straight ahead).

◆ **tha to dite** you will see it. **To** (it) refers to the tourist office, which is neuter, but if you are talking about the bank, **i trápeza** (feminine), you would say **tha ti dite**. Both these phrases are in the future. Another useful phrase is **pou ine i astinomia tourismoú?** (where is the tourist police?).

6 *Vivi is looking for the bus stop*

Vivi	Parakaló pou ine i stasi tou leoforíou?
Maria	Ine ekí apénandi.
Vivi	Efharistó.
Maria	Parakaló.

7 *On the bus. This woman doesn't know where to get off for Platia Sintágmatos (Constitution Square), so another traveller helps her*

Mia taksidiótisa	Signomi kiria, se piá stasi prepi na katevo yiá tin Platia Sintágmatos?
Ali taksidiótisa	Tha periménete ligo, tha katevo ke'egó ekí, ine tris stasis akomi ap'edó.
Mia taksidiótisa	Efharistó.
Ali taksidístisa	Parakaló.

i taksidiótisa passenger (woman)
ali another (f.)

8 *Jimi wants to telephone London, but where is the OTE?*

Jimi	Pou ine to OTE parakaló, yiatí thelo na tilefoniso sto Londino.
Kiria	Tha perpatísete liga metra, ke sto proto stenó aristerá, tha to dite.
Jimi	Efharistó.

OTE Telecommunications Organization of Greece. See *Did you know?*

9 *Eleni has lost her way to the Hotel Coral*

Eleni	Parakaló, pou ine to ksenodohio Coral?
Marina	To ksenodohio Coral ine kondá stin paralia, tha prohorísete ísia brostá.
Eleni	Efharistó.
Marina	Parakaló.

i paralia sea front

6 ♦ **i stasi tou leoforiou** the bus stop (lit. the stop of the bus). **To leoforio** (the bus) changes to **tou leoforiou** (of the bus). Remember **Avgoustos** (August) **15 Avgoustou** (August 15) in Unit 4, dialogue 8.

♦ **ine ekí apénandi** it's there across the street.

7 ♦ **se piá stasi?** at which stop?

♦ **prepi na katevo** must I get off. **Prepi** means 'it is necessary/must/ought': it is a very useful word and easy to use since you don't have to change the ending e.g. **prepi na pao** (I must go), **prepi na kánoune** (they must do) etc. Don't forget to put **na** to link **prepi** with the following verb.

♦ **yiá tin Platia Sintágmatos** for Constitution Square. As with **apó** (from) and **me** (with), after **yiá** (for) **i** changes to **ti(n)**. Here are some other examples: **yiá ti yineka** (for the woman), **yiá tin Athina** (for Athens), **yiá ti Glyfada** (for Glyfada).

tha periménete ligo you'll have to wait a little (lit. you will wait a little).

tha katevo k'egó ekí I'm getting off there too. Here is another example of **ke** meaning 'too/as well' rather than 'and'. In speech when **ke** comes before a vowel it runs into the following word; so **ke + egó = k'egó** (I/me too).

ine tris stasis akomi ap'edó it's three stops more from here. **Apó + edó = ap'edó** (from here).

8 **yiatí thelo na tilefoniso** because I want to telephone. **Yiatí?** (with a questioning intonation) means 'why?' As you can see, the word is made from **yiá** (for) and **ti?** (what?). Note again how **na** is used to link the two verbs.

♦ **tha perpatísete liga metra** you should walk a few meters (lit. you will walk . . .).

♦ **ke sto proto stenó aristerá** and at the first side street on the left.

tha to dite you'll see it.

9 **ine kondá stin paralia** it is near to the sea shore/waterfront.

tha prohorísete ísia brostá you should go straight ahead (lit. you will proceed straight forward).

| | **10** | *Once again kiria Anna is looking for the post office* |

Kiria Anna   Kírie sas parakaló, to tahidromio?
Kírios   Ne, tha katevite efthían, ke tha strípesete aristerá.
Kiria Anna   Ah! Efharistó polí.

| | **11** | *Kiria Anna wants to know where Akadimia Street is* |

Kiria Anna   Sas parakaló, borite na mou pite pou ine i odós Akadimias?
Kírios   Ne, kiria mou; efthian sto trito stenó, deksiá tha strípsete.
Kiria Anna   Borite na to epanalávete?
Kírios   Ne pos, efthían sto trito stenó deksiá.
Kiria Anna   Ah! Efharistó polí.
Kírios   Parakaló.

| | **12** | *The manager's son is still doing his arithmetic while his mother makes arrangements to go out with a friend* |

Pedí   ekatón deka (110), ekatón íkosi (120), ekatón trianda (130), ekatón saranda (140), ekatón peninda (150), ekatón eksinda (160), ekatón evdominda (170) ekatón egdonda (180), ekatón eneninda (190), diakosa (200), diakosa deka (210), diakosa íkosi (220), diakosa trianda (230), diakosa saranda (240), diakosa peninda (250), diakosa eksinda (260), diakosa evdominda (270), diakosa ogdonda (280), diakosa eneninda (290) trakosa (300), trakosa deka (310), trakosa íkosi (320), trakosa trianda (330), trakosa saranda (340), trakosa peninda (350), trakosa eksinda (360), trakosa evdominda (370), trakosa ogdanda (380), trakosa eneninda (390), tetrakosa (400), tetrakosa deka (410), tetrakosa íkosi (420), tetrakosa trianda (430), tetrakosa saranda (440), tetrakosa peninda (450), tetrakosa eksinda (460), tetrakosa evdominda (470) tetrakosa ogdonda (480), tetrakosa eneninda (490) pendakosa (500).

Sofia   Apopse to vradi leo na pame stin Kifissia, ine mono deka pende hiliómetra makriá, ke ehi para polí orees tavernes. Thelis?
Eleni   Pame, pame, esí?
Pedí   Thelo.

10   **tha katevite** you should go down (lit. you will descend).

       efthian straight ahead. **Efthia/efthian** are alternative ways of saying **ísia brostá**.

       tha strípsete you should turn (lit. you will turn).

11   **borite na mou pite** can you tell me.

    ♦ **pou ine i odós Akadimias?** where is Akadimia Street? We have seen how **Avgoustos** (August) became **Avgoustou** (of August) and **leoforio** (bus) became **leoforiou** (of the bus) by changing the endings to **-ou**. The ending **-ou** is used for 'of' for masculine and neuter nouns; to add the 'of' to feminine nouns we simply add an **-s** to the end of the word. So, **Akadimia** (Academy), **Akadimias** (of the Academy), **i odós Akadimias** Academy Street (lit. the street of the Academy).

    ♦ **borite na to epanalávete?** can you repeat that?

       ne pos yes certainly.

12   **apopse to vradi** this evening (lit. tonight in the evening).

       leo na pame I say we should go (lit. I say let's go).

       stin Kifissia to Kifissia. Do you remember **sto Londino** to London? (**se + to = sto**). Here it is **se + ti(n) = stin** because Kifissia is feminine.

       ine mono deka pende h116metra makriá it's only 15 kilometers away. Using **kondá** (near) and **makriá** (far) you can ask questions like these: **ine makriá** (is it far?) and **ine kondá** (is it near?).

       ehi para polí (orees tavernes) it has very, very (nice tavernas). The **para** makes the **polí** stronger e.g. **efharistó para polí** (thank you *so* much).

    ♦ **pame** let's go; e.g. **pame sto sinemá** (let's go to the cinema), **pame stin plaz** (let's go to the beach).

Key words and phrases

To learn

signomi	excuse me, sorry
pou ine i trápeza?	where is the bank?
to tahidromio?	the post office?
to farmakio?	the pharmacy?
to touristikó grafio?	the tourist office?
to ksenodohio?	the hotel?
i toualeta?	the toilet?
i paralia?	the waterfront?

iparhi mia taverna edó kondá?	is there a taverna near here?
pou ine i stasi tou leoforiou?	where is the bus stop?
se piá stasi prepi na katevo?	at which stop must I get off?
borite na to epanalávete?	could you repeat it?

ekató	100
ekató peninda	150
diakosa	200
diakosa deka	210
diakosa trianda	230
trakosa	300
trakosa deka	310
trakosa íkosi	320
tetrakosa	400
tetrakosa íkosi	420
tetrakosa peninda	450
pendakosa	500

To understand

apénandi	facing, across the street
diakosa metra	200 meters
aristerá	left
deksiá	right
ísia brostá	straight ahead
efthia/efthian	straight ahead
proto stenó	first street
dio stasis apó edó	two stops from here
deka pende hiliómetra	15 kilometers
sto vathos	at the back
tha periménete	you should wait
tha perpatísete	you should walk
tha pate	you should go
tha katevite	you should get off
tha strípsete	you should turn
tha to dite	you'll see it
pame	let's go

Practice what you have learned

Remember to read the instructions to each exercise before switching on the tape.

1 Listen to the tape and mark in the appropriate box the directions given for each place.

aristerá	efthia	deksiá	
		✓	Pou ine i trápeza?
	✓		Pou ine to tahidromio?
✓			Pou ine to mousio?
		✓	Pou ine i stasi tou leoforiou?
	✓		Pou ine to farmakio?
	✓		Pou ine i Akrópoli?

2 Starting from the point indicated, follow the directions and write down where you get to. Listen to the tape and check your answers.

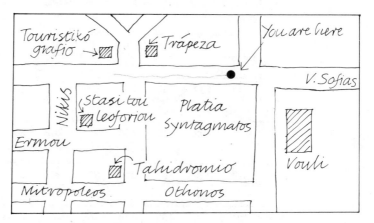

a. Tha pate ísia brostá ke tha to dite. Ine to touristikó grafio.

b. Tha pate ísia brostá ke tha strípsete aristerá, sto déftero stenó tha to dite. Ine to _tahidromio_

c. Tha pate ísia brostá ke tha strípsete aristerá, sto proto stenó tha ti dite. Ine i _stasi tou leoforiou_

d. Tha pate ísia brostá, sto touristikó grafio apénandi tha ti dite.
Ine i _trapeza_

3 Follow the example and match the questions from below with the appropriate replies. Then check your answers with the tape and translate all four exchanges into English. (Answers p. 76)

a. *Eleni* To tahidromio ine makriá?
    Petros Ohi, ine kondá.
b. *Eleni* ~~Povi la javri~~
    Petros Ine edó apénandi.
c. *Petros* ~~Ine i Akr~~
    Eleni Ne, i Akropoli ine polí makriá
d. *Eleni* ~~Pou prepo na katevo yiá tin Akropoli~~
    Petros Stin próti stasi.

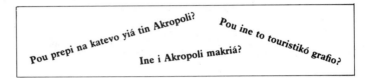

Pou prepi na katevo yiá tin Akropoli?

Pou ine to touristikó grafio?

Ine i Akropoli makriá?

4 Listen to the tape and tick the numbers you hear. They correspond to all the rooms which are taken in this hotel. (Answers p. 76)

	1	2	3	4	5	6	7	8	9
		✓		✓		✓			✓
100	101	102	103	104	105	106	107	108	109
		✓	✓				✓		
200	201	202	203	204	205	206	207	208	209
						✓	✓		✓
300	301	302	303	304	305	306	307	308	309
						✓			
400	401	402	403	404	405	406	407	408	409
✓					✓				
500	501	502	503	504	505	506	507	508	509
✓									

Grammar

Making nouns plural

To make nouns plural you have to change their endings: masculine nouns in the plural end in **-i** or **-es**, feminine nouns in **-es** and neuter nouns in **-a**. The word for 'the' also changes from the singular forms **o**, **i**, **to**, to the plural forms **i**, **i**, **ta**:

o andras	man	**i andres**	men (m.)
o stathmós	station	**i stathmí**	stations (m.)
i yineka	woman	**i yinekes**	women (f.)
i karekla	chair	**i karekles**	chairs (f.)
to pedí	child	**ta pediá**	children (n.)
to domátio	room	**ta domátia**	rooms (n.)

Pao

The verb to note in this unit is **pao** (I go)

pao	I go	**pame**	we go
pas	you go	**pate**	you go
pai	he/she/it goes	**pane**	they go

Exercise 1

Write the appropriate words under each picture. Follow the example (Answers p. 76)

a. *i andres*   b. *i yinekes*   c. *i karekles*

d. *ta lemonia*   e. *ta psomia*   f. *ta ksenodohia*

Exercise 2

Write the plural of the following nouns, and translate them. (Answers p. 76)

a. to domátio *ta domatia*

b. to diavatírio *ta diavatiria*

c. to avgó *ta avgá*

d. i tirópita *i tiropites*

e. o stathmós *i stathmi*

f. i trápeza *i trápezes*

UNIT 5

73

The Greek alphabet

Letters you have already met

A α	'a' as in father	K κ	'k' as in key
Δ δ	'd' as in door	M μ	'm' as in my
E ε	'e' as in let	T τ	't' as in tip
I ι	'i' as in police	Φ φ	'f' as in four

New letters

Letter	Name	Equivalent sound in English
Σ σ ς*	sigma	's' as in send
Π π	pi	'p' as in pie

*only at the end of words

First cover the left-hand column and underline the new letters. Then uncover it and read the words out loud.

parakaló	παρακαλῶ
símera	σήμερα
se	σέ
pagotó	παγωτό
paralia	παραλία
apó	ἀπό
sas	σας
spanakópita	σπανακόπιτα
peraste	περάστε
signomi	συγγνώμη

Exercise

Here you have four words, **tahidromio, farmakio, odós** and **trápeza**; copy each one once and translate them. (Answers p. 76)

a. ΤΑΧΥΔΡΟΜΕΙΟ .... *ΤαχyΔΡΟΜΕΙΟ* ....

b. ΦΑΡΜΑΚΕΙΟ .... *ΦΑΡΜΑΚΕΙΟ* ....

c. ΟΔΟΣ .... *ΟΔΟΣ* ....

d. ΤΡΑΠΕΖΑ .... *ΤΡΑΠΕΖΑ* ....

Did you know?

Information about Greece

In the main centers there are tourist information offices which offer a wide-ranging service including recommending accommodations and giving time-table information. You can get their addresses from the Greek National Tourist Office, Olympic Tower, 645 5th Ave., New York, N.Y. 10022. There is also a section of the Greek police – the Tourist Police – whose job it is to assist visitors generally, to control prices and deal with complaints. Many Tourist Police officers speak English.

The post office

There are post offices in nearly all towns and villages. Opening times are displayed outside but are usually from 8 a.m. to 1 p.m.; newsstands and hotels also sell stamps. For General Delivery, you should show your passport at the counter marked ΠΟΣΤ ΡΕΣΤΑΝΤ at the town's main post office. Mail boxes are yellow.

Telephoning

The telephone system is run by the Greek Telecommunications Organization (**OTE**). **OTE** has offices all over Greece where you can make local and international calls. You pay for your calls afterwards, so you don't need a pocketful of change. The number of public phones in Greece is rather limited. However, almost all newsstands and a number of cafés have phones for the public. These phones have meters and you pay after phoning according to the number of units used. The few public telephone booths are blue for local calls and orange for long distance and take coins not tokens. If you do use a telephone directory (written in Greek script, of course) it is useful to note that each town or island is listed separately with the subscribers in alphabetical order.

Your turn to speak

Read the introduction to the two exercises and then work with the tape alone. You are going to practice asking whether a place is far away, **ine makriá**, or nearby, **edó kondá**, and then what to say if you don't understand – **den katálava**. And finally, you're going to take the bus and find out where to get off, **se piá stasi prepi na katevo?**

1 You have just arrived in Greece and can't wait to get to the beach, **i paralia**, but where is it? Afterwards you want to send a card home, so where's the post office?

2 You've had too much sun, so before going to the Akropolis you need a pharmacy, **to farmakio**, and then the bus stop, **i stasi**.

Answers

Practice what you have learned p. 72 Exercise **3** (**a**) Is the post office far? No, it is near (**b**) Where is the tourist office? It is here across the street (**c**) Is the Akropolis far? Yes the Akropolis is very far (**d**) Where must I get off for the Akropolis? At the first stop.

p. 72 Exercise **4** 2, 4, 6, 9, 102, 103, 107, 206, 207, 209, 306, 400, 405, 500.

Grammar p. 73 Exercise **1** (**b**) i yinekes (**c**) i karekles (**d**) ta lemónia (**e**) ta psomiá (**f**) ta ksenodohia.

p. 73 Exercise **2** (**a**) ta domátia, the rooms (**b**) ta diavatíria, the passports (**c**) ta avgá, the eggs (**d**) i tirópites, the cheese pies (**e**) i stathmí, the stations (**f**) i trápezes, the banks.

The Greek alphabet p. 74 (**a**) Post office (**b**) Pharmacy (**c**) Street (**d**) Bank.

UNIT 5

6 Time

You will learn

- to inquire what the time is
- to tell time
- to ask when planes, boats etc. leave
- to ask and understand when shops and banks open and close
- the days of the week and months of the year

Do you remember?

is there a bank nearby?   **iparhi mia trápeza edó kondá?**
the third street on the right   **trito steno deksiá**

Before you begin

Follow the pattern of study set out in the *Study guide* below. Work steadily
through the unit and mark off each section as you complete it.

Study guide

	Dialogues 1–3: listen without the book
	Dialogues 1–3: listen, read and study one by one
	Dialogues 4–6: listen without the book
	Dialogues 4–6: listen, read and study one by one
	Dialogues 7, 8: listen without the book
	Dialogues 7, 8: listen, read and study one by one
	Dialogues 9, 10: listen without the book
	Dialogues 9, 10: listen, read and study one by one
	Study *Key words and phrases*
	Complete the exercises in *Practice what you have learned*
	Study *Grammar* and do the exercise
	Do *The Greek alphabet* and complete the exercise
	Read *Did you know?*
	Do the taped exercises in *Your turn to speak*
	Listen to all the dialogues again
	Finally, do *Revision/Review Units 4–6* at the end of the book

Dialogues

1 *Eleni wants to know the time*

Eleni Signomi, mipos éhete ora?
Maria Ne, eho.
Eleni Ti ora ine?
Maria Ine dódeka.
Eleni Efharistó.
Maria Parakaló.

2 *At the airport. What time does the plane leave for Mykonos?*

Kiria Parakaló, ti ora fevyi to aeroplano yiá Mykono?
Ipálilos Ne, ena leptó. Fevyi símera stis deka to proí.
Kiria Endaksi. Efharistó.
Ipálilos Parakaló

to aeroplano plane
to proí morning

3 *Katerina has just arrived at her hotel and wants to know the times of the meals*

Katerina Ti ora servírete to proinó sto ksenodohio?
Ipálilos To proinó servírete metaksí eftámisi ke eneámisi.
Katerina Ke ta ala yévmata?
Ipálilos To mesimerianó ine dódeka me dio, ke to vradinó ine eftá me enea.

4 *Two children are learning the days of the week and the months of the year*

Dina Kiriakí, Deftera, Triti, Tetarti, Pempti, Paraskeví, Sávato.

Nina Ianouários, Fevrouários, Mártios, Aprílios, Máios, Ioúnios, Ioúlios, Ávgoustos, Septémvrios, Októvrios, Noémvrios ke Dekémvrios.

1 mipos éhete ora? I wonder, have you got the time? **Mipos** has the tentative meaning 'I wonder/perhaps. . .' and is a very useful polite opening to a question. **Ora** in Greek means both the hour of the day and time generally e.g. **den eho ora** (I haven't got time).

♦ **ti ora ine?** what time is it?

ine dódeka it's twelve. You could say **ine dódeka i ora** (it's 12 o'clock).

2 ♦ **ti ora fevyi to aeroplano?** what time does the plane leave? Here are some other examples: **ti ora fevyi to treno/to plio/to poulman/to leoforio?** (what time does the train/boat/coach/bus leave?).

♦ **fevyi símera stis deka to proí** it leaves today at ten o'clock in the morning. 'At ten o'clock in the evening' is **stis deka to vradi**. To say 'at . . . o'clock', simply use **stis** + the number e.g. **stis dio** (at two), **stis éndeka** (at eleven). The only exception is **sti mia** (at one), which is **sti** rather than **stis** because it is singular.

3 ♦ **ti ora servírete to proinó?** what time is breakfast served?

♦ **metaksí eftámisi ke eneámisi** between half past seven and half past nine. The word for half is **misí**: you can either add it directly to the number, as above, or insert a **ke** e.g. **mia ke misí** (half past one, lit. one and a half) or **miámisi**.

ke ta ala yévmata? and the other meals? 'Meal' is a neuter noun **to yevma**: so, **to alo yevma** (the other meal), **ta ala yevmata** (the other meals).

♦ **to mesimerianó ine dódeka me dio** lunch is from twelve to two. **Mesimeri** means 'midday', so the word **mesimerianó** (lunch) comes from **to mesimerianó (yevma)** = the midday (meal). Here we see another use of **me** to mean 'from . . . until. . .'

ke to vradinó ine eftá me enea and dinner is from seven to nine. 'The evening' is **to vradi**, so **to vradinó (yevma)** = the evening (meal) i.e. dinner.

4 ♦ the days of the week are all feminine except Saturday, **Sávato**, which is neuter. If you want to say 'on Friday' you should say **tin Paraskeví**, but for Saturday it's **to Sávato**. Note that the first day of the week is Sunday.

♦ all the months of the year are masculine and if you want to say, for example, 'in December' it is **to Dekemvrio**, without the last 's'. As in English, the days of the week and the months of the year are written with capital letters. Learn them all off by heart.

5 *Eleni is very forgetful, what day is it today?*

Eleni	Ti mera éhoume símera?
Maria	Símera ine Deftera.
Eleni	Ti mina?
Maria	Ioulio.
Eleni	Efharistó.
Maria	Parakaló.

o minas month

6 *At the port of Piraeus. When is there a boat for Idra?*

Tourístria	Signomi parakaló, pote fevyi to plio yiá tin Idra?
Ipálilos	Ehi stis enea ke stis diómisi ke kathe Triti, Pempti ke Sávato stis októ, stis enea ke stis diómisi.
Tourístria	Efharistó.
Ipálilos	Parakaló.

kathe every

7 *What is the latest time to get to the airport?*

Tourístria	Signomi, ti ora prepi na ime sto aerodrómio?
Ipálilos	Prepi na iste sto aerodrómio stis eftá to argótero.
Tourístria	Efharistó.
Ipálilos	Parakaló.

5 ♦ **ti mera éhoume símera?** what day is it today? (lit. what day do we have today?).

ti mina? what month? The plural of **mina** is **mines**.

6 ♦ **pote fevyi to plio yiá tin Idra?** when does the boat leave for Idra (Hydra)? Remember that after **yiá** (for) the feminine **i** changes to **ti(n)**.

ehi stis enea ke stis diómisi there is one at nine and at half past two. **Ehi** means literally 'he/she/it has' but is also used for 'there is. . .'

♦ **ke kathe Triti, Pempti ke Savato** and every Tuesday, Thursday and Saturday.

7 ♦ **ti ora prepi na ime sto aerodrómio?** what time must I be at the airport? Remember from Unit 5, dialogue 7 that the verb **prepi** (it is necessary/must/ought) does not change for different persons.

prepi na íste you must be.

stis eftá to argótero at seven (at) the latest. Making words of comparison in Greek is very straightforward e.g. **argá** (late), **argótero** (later), **to argótero** (the latest); **kaló** (good), **kalítero** (better), **to kalítero** (the best). You will notice that the last letter of the words changes when **-tero** is added; don't worry about this, the important thing at this stage is to recognize the endings.

8 *Katerina is inquiring about times again. Here she's asking about the shops*

Katerina   Ta katastímata stin Ellada ti ora anigoun to proí, ke ti ora anigoun to apóyevma?
Maria   To proí anígoune stis októmisi ke to apóyevma stis pende.
Katerina   Ke piés ores klinoun?
Maria   Yiá mesimeri klinoune stis diómisi ke to vradi klínoune stis októ.

to apóyevma afternoon, in the afternoon
to mesimeri midday
aniktó open
klistó closed

9 *A friend invites Anna for a ride in his car*

Yiorgos   Ti kanis apopse?
Anna   Típota idiétero.
Yiorgos   Pame mia volta me to aftokinitó mou?
Anna   Kalí idea.
Yiorgos   Piá ine i kalíteri ora na sinantithoume?
Anna   Yiro stis eptá.
Yiorgos   Málista.
Anna   Endaksi.

to aftokínito car
i idea idea

10 *It's a lovely day, but Eleni doesn't realize that it's Greek Independence Day, March 25*

Eleni   Kalimera.
Sofia   Ti kanis?
Eleni   Kalá efharistó, k'esí?
Sofia   Polí oréa, ine símera mia para polí oréa mera.
Eleni   Ti ine símera?
Sofia   Ikosipempti Martiou.
Eleni   Deftera?
Sofia   Triti, Triti. Triti ine! Triti!

8 ◆ **ti ora anigoun ta katastímata?** what time do the shops open? But if you want to know at what time one shop opens it is **aniyi** e.g. **ti ora aniyi to farmakio?** (what time does the pharmacy open?). **Ta katastímata** is the plural of the neuter noun **to katástima** (the store, the shop).

piés ores klinoun? when do they close? (lit. which hours do they close?).

klinoune they close. Note that for 'they' you can use the verb with **e** at the end or without, here are some examples: **anigoun** or **anígoune** (they open), **klinoun** or **klínoune** (they close) **milán** or **milane** (they speak).

9 ◆ **ti kanis apopse?** what are you doing tonight? He uses the familiar form, but to be formal you would say **kánete.**

típota idiétero nothing special.

◆ **pame mia volta me to aftokinitó mou** let's go for a ride in my car. **Volta** can also mean 'a stroll'.

◆ **piá ine i kalíteri ora na sinantithoume?** what is the best time to meet? Do you remember from dialogue 7 the ending **-tero** (= -er)? In this case the ending is **-teri** because they are speaking about something feminine, **i ora** (the time).

◆ **yiro stis eptá** around seven. Remember to use **stis** before your times.

The Greeks sometimes jokingly refer to on-the-dot punctuality as **anglikí ora** (English time) as opposed to their own rather more relaxed and haphazard time-keeping **ellinikí ora** (Greek time).

10 **mia para polí orea mera** a very, very lovely day. Remember how the **para** makes the **polí** more emphatic (Unit 5, dialogue 13).

Key words and phrases

To learn

ti ora ine?	what time is it?
ti ora servírete to proinó?	what time is breakfast served?
to mesimerianó?	lunch served?
to vradinó?	dinner served?
ti ora fevyi to plio?	what time does the boat leave?
to treno?	train leave?
to leoforio?	bus leave?
to poulman?	coach leave?
pote fevyi to aeroplano yiá. . ?	what time does the plane leave for. . ?
ti ora prepi na ime sto	what time must I be at the
aerodrómio?	airport?
sto limani?	the port?
piá mera fevyi. . ?	what day does . . . leave?
ti mera éhoume símera?	what day is it today?
ti ora anigoun ta katastímata?	what time do the shops open?
klinoun ta katastímata?	close?

To understand

Note: times not on the hour are explained in *Grammar* p. 87.

ine deka akrivós	it is ten o'clock precisely
ine deka ke pende	it is five past ten
ine deka ke tétarto	it is a quarter past ten
ine deka ke misí	it is half past ten
ine éndeka para íkosi	it is twenty to eleven
ine éndeka para tétarto	it is a quarter to eleven
metaksí eftámisi ke eneámisi	between half past seven and half past nine
dódeka me dio	from twelve until two
kathe Triti	every Tuesday
yiro stis eftá	about seven
ti kanis/kánete apopse?	what are you doing tonight?
pame mia volta	let's go for a stroll/drive

Days of the week

i Kiriakí	Sunday
i Deftera	Monday
i Triti	Tuesday
i Tetarti	Wednesday
i Pempti	Thursday
i Paraskeví	Friday
to Savato	Saturday

Months of the year

Ianouários	January	Ioúlios	July
Fevrouários	February	Ávgoustos	August
Mártios	March	Septémvrios	September
Aprílios	April	Októvrios	October
Máios	May	Noémvrios	November
Ioúnios	June	Dekémvrios	December

Practice what you have learned

1 Listen to the tape and then complete this list of mealtimes at your hotel. (Answers p. 90)

	from	until
Breakfast	7	10:00
Lunch	12	2:30
Dinner	8	9:30

2 Listen to the tape, then note down the date that people will arrive and will leave their hotel. (Answers p. 90)

	arrival	departure
Dendrinos	13 March	30 March
Mavraki	1 May	15 May
Spirotopoulos	8 July	22 July

3 In this boat timetable the times are missing. Listen to the tape and complete them. (Answers p. 90)

Vessel	Time	Destination
Minos	6	Iraklion (Kriti)
Naias	8	Syros, Tinos, Mykonos
Limnos	8	Paros, Naxos, Thira
Knossos	630	Iraklion (Kriti)
Kriti	8:30	Chania (Kriti)

ΙΑΝΟΥΑΡΙΟΣ	ΦΕΒΡΟΥΑΡΙΟΣ	ΜΑΡΤΙΟΣ	ΙΟΥΛΙΟΣ	ΑΥΓΟΥΣΤΟΣ	ΣΕΠΤΕΜΒΡΙΟΣ
Κ 4 11 18 25	1 8 15 22	1 8 15 22 29	Κ 5 12 19 26	2 9 16 23 30	6 13 20 27
Δ 5 12 19 26	2 9 16 23	2 9 16 23 30	Δ 6 13 20 27	3 10 17 24 31	7 14 21 28
Τ 6 13 20 27	3 10 17 24	3 10 17 24 31	Τ 7 14 21 28	4 11 18 25	1 8 15 22 29
Τ 7 14 21 28	4 11 18 25	4 11 18 25	Τ 1 8 15 22 29	5 12 19 26	2 9 16 23 30
Π 1 8 15 22 29	5 12 19 26	5 12 19 26	Π 2 9 16 23 30	6 13 20 27	3 10 17 24
Π 2 9 16 23 30	6 13 20 27	6 13 20 27	Π 3 10 17 24 31	7 14 21 28	4 11 18 25
Σ 3 10 17 24 31	7 14 21 28	7 14 21 28	Σ 4 11 18 25	1 8 15 22 29	5 12 19 26

ΑΠΡΙΛΙΟΣ	ΜΑΪΟΣ	ΙΟΥΝΙΟΣ	ΟΚΤΩΒΡΙΟΣ	ΝΟΕΜΒΡΙΟΣ	ΔΕΚΕΜΒΡΙΟΣ
Κ 5 12 19 26	3 10 17 24 31	7 14 21 28	Κ 4 11 18 25	1 8 15 22 29	6 13 20 27
Δ 6 13 20 27	4 11 18 25	1 8 15 22 29	Δ 5 12 19 26	2 9 16 23 30	7 14 21 28
Τ 7 14 21 28	5 12 19 26	2 9 16 23 30	Τ 6 13 20 27	3 10 17 24	1 8 15 22 29
Τ 1 8 15 22 29	6 13 20 27	3 10 17 24	Τ 7 14 21 28	4 11 18 25	2 9 16 23 30
Π 2 9 16 23 30	7 14 21 28	4 11 18 25	Π 1 8 15 22 29	5 12 19 26	3 10 17 24 31
Π 3 10 17 24	1 8 15 22 29	5 12 19 26	Π 2 9 16 23 30	6 13 20 27	4 11 18 25
Σ 4 11 18 25	2 9 16 23 30	6 13 20 27	Σ 3 10 17 24 31	7 14 21 28	5 12 19 26

4 Listen to the tape and tick the correct answers. (Answers p. 90)

1 Ti ora anigoun ta katastímata?
a. ☐ stis októ
b. ☒ stis októmisi
c. ☐ sti mia

2 To ora aniyi to farmakio?
a. ☐ stis eftá
b. ☒ stis októ
c. ☐ stis deka ke misí

3 Ti ora klini to farmakio?
a. ☐ stis dódeka
b. ☐ sti mia
c. ☒ stis diómisi

4 Ti ora klinoun yiá mesimeri ta katastímata?
a. ☐ stis dio
b. ☐ sti mia
c. ☒ stis diómisi

5 Ti ora anigoun to apóyevma?
a. ☐ stis tris
b. ☒ stis pende
c. ☐ stis pende ke misí

6 Ti ora klinoune to vradi?
a. ☐ stis deka
b. ☒ stis októmisi
c. ☐ stis októ

Grammar

Telling time

Ti ora ine? what time is it?
Telling time is quite straightforward in Greek, you put the hours first
followed by **ke** (plus) or **pará** (minus) the minutes. Here are some
examples:

ine pende or **ine pende i ora** it's five o'clock
ine pende ke deka it's ten past five
ine pende ke tétarto it's a quarter past five
ine pende ke misí it's half past five
ine eksi pará tétarto it's a quarter to six

You may need to say whether the time is morning or evening:
októ to proí eight in the morning
októ to vradi eight in the evening
dódeka to mesimeri 12 midday
dódeka ti nihta 12 midnight
ti ora fevyi to aeroplano yiá Mykono? what time does the plane
leave for Mykonos?
fevyi stis deka to proí it leaves at ten o'clock in the morning
Note how to say 'at ten o'clock'   **stis deka**
                  'at five o'clock'   **stis pende**
          but   'at one o'clock'   **sti mia**

When you need to insist on precision use **akrivós** (precisely), 'at seven
o'clock precisely' **stis eftá akrivós.** But if you want to give a rough idea
use **yiro** (about/around), 'about nine o'clock' **yiro stis enea.**

Fevgo

Here are three more common verbs: **fevgo** (I leave), **anigo** (I open) and
klino (I close). Here is **fevgo,** the others follow the same pattern.

fevgo	I leave	**févgoume**	we leave
fevyis	you leave	**févyete**	you leave
fevyi	he/she/it leaves	**févgoune**	they leave

Exercise   Write down the times indicated on the clocks below in full. (Answers p. 90)

Ti ora ine?

Ine. . .

a. *ine tria akrivós*   b. *ine tesera ke pende*   c. *ine pende ke deka*   d. *in eksi para tetarto*

e. *ine deka ka deka*   f. *ine mia para penda*   g. *ine triamisa*   h. *in efta para ikosi*

The Greek alphabet

Letters you have already met

A α	'a' as in father	M μ	'm' as in my
Δ δ	'd' as in door	Π π	'p' as in pie
E ε	'e' as in let	Σ σ ς	's' as in send
I ι	'i' as in police	T τ	't' as in tip
K κ	'k' as in key	Φ φ	'f' as in four

New letters

Letter	Name	Equivalent sound in English
B β	vita	'v' as in van
Ω ω	omega	'o' as in hot

First cover the left-hand column and underline the new letters.
Then uncover it and read the words out loud.

ora	ὥρα
os	ὡς
vathos	βάθως
vradi	βράδι
vradinó	βραδινό
volta	βόλτα
vísino	βύσσινο
voútiro	βούτιρο
orea	ὡραῖα
valitsa	βαλίτσα

Did you know?

Public holidays

As well as on the religious holidays described below, shops and offices are closed on Christmas (not recognized as a religious holiday in Greece) and on the first weekday after Christmas, as well as on the following secular public holidays:

January 1 (**Protohroniá**)
March 25 (Greek Independence Day)
May 1 (**Protomayiá**)
October 28 (**Ohi** Day). The **ohi** (no!) refers to Greece's one word reply to Mussolini's ultimatum in 1940 which brought the country into the war.

Religious holidays

The vast majority of Greeks belong to the Greek Orthodox Church. There are small minorities of other denominations and religions including Catholics (mainly in Syros, Tinos and Corfu) and Muslims (in Thrace). Orthodox priests can be recognized by their long black robes, beards and tall black hats. Ordinary parish priests can marry but monks, from among whom bishops are selected, cannot. The most important festival, both religious and social, is Easter. As a different religious calendar is used Greek Easter seldom coincides with Western Easter. Many Greeks fast during Lent and virtually everybody carries lighted candles to church on Good Friday and attends the Resurrection Service on Easter Saturday which reaches its climax at midnight. At the end of the service, bells are rung and fireworks let off and people return home to eat **mayiritsa**, a special soup made of lambs' offal. On Easter Sunday families celebrate with a feast of roast lamb cooked in the open air.

Two other important festivals are Clean Monday (**Katharí Deftera**) at the beginning of Lent which is preceded by a period of carnival, and the Assumption of the Virgin Mary on August 15. During all these celebrations, buses, boats and planes are crowded so it's advisable to book well in advance. Tavernas and restaurants are also very busy and it's best to reserve a table if you can.

Your turn to speak

Read the instructions for each exercise separately and then work with the tape alone. You are going to practice asking questions about time.

1   You are very tired after your long journey but before you go to sleep you want to know what time things happen in your hotel. You will use **ti ora? ti ora aniyi? ti ora klini?**

2   You want to go to Mykonos but you don't know the timetable of the boats. You will use **piá mera? ti ora fevyi? proí, apóyevma** and **vradi.**

Piraeus

Revision/Review

Now turn to p. 215 and complete the revision section on Units 4–6. On the cassette *Revision* follows after this unit.

Answers

Practice what you have learned p. 85 Exercise 1 7:00–10:00, 12:00–2:30, 8:00–9:30.

p. 85 Exercise 2 Dendrinos March 13–March 30; Mavraki May 1–May 15; Spirotopoulos July 8–July 22.

p. 85 Exercise 3 *Minos* 6:00; *Naias* 8:00; *Limnos* 8:00; *Knossos* 6:30; *Kriti* 8:30.

p. 86 Exercise 4 1b, 2b, 3c, 4c, 5b, 6b.

Grammar p. 87 (a) tris akrivós   (b) tésseris ke pende   (c) pende ke deka (d) eksi pará tétarto   (e) deka ke deka   (f) mia pará pende   (g) tris ke misí   (h) eftá pará íkosi.

7 Shopping – Part 1

You will learn

- to ask for what you need at the newsstand, the general store, the bakery and the post office
- to describe in more detail what you want to buy
- to understand shopkeepers' questions
- to ask the price of an article
- numbers 500–1,000
- to read some common signs in Greek

Do you remember?

what time is breakfast served?	**ti ora servírete to prionó?**
what time do the shops close?	**ti ora klinoun ta katastímata?**
on Sunday at ten o'clock	**tin Kiriakí stis deka**

Before you begin

Follow the pattern of study set out in the *Study guide* below. Don't be afraid to go over things again or vary the order to suit yourself.

Study guide

	Dialogues 1–3: listen without the book
	Dialogues 1–3: listen, read and study one by one
	Dialogues 4–6: listen without the book
	Dialogues 4–6: listen, read and study one by one
	Dialogues 7, 8: listen without the book
	Dialogues 7, 8: listen, read and study one by one
	Study *Key words and phrases*
	Complete the exercises in *Practice what you have learned*
	Study *Grammar* and do the exercise
	Do *The Greek alphabet* and complete the exercise
	Read *Did you know?*
	Do the taped exercises in *Your turn to speak*
	Finally, listen to all the dialogues again

Dialogues

1 *A little boy is buying at the baker's (**o fournos**)*

Pedí	Ena kiló frandzola, parakaló.
Ipálilos	Ne.
Pedí	Mia frandzola.
Ipálilos	Ti alo?
Pedí	Aftá.
Ipálilos	Íkosi drahmés.
Pedí	Efharistó polí.

i frandzola French loaf
to kilo kilogram

2 *A woman buys some matches*

Kiria	Thelo ena koutí spirta.
Ipálilos	Mikró i megalo?
Kiria	Megalo.
Ipálilos	Oriste.
Kiria	Efharistó.
Ipálilos	Parakaló.

3 *At a newsstand (**to períptero**)*

Vasiliki	Éhete grammatósima?
Kírios	Eho, yiá pou thelis?
Vasiliki	Yiá tin Anglia.
Kírios	Yiá tin Anglia ehi, pos. Dekatésseres drahmés.
Vasiliki	Endaksi, doste mou ena.

1 ♦ **ena kiló** a kilo, (in Greece bread is bought by weight). Using **ena kiló**, **miso kiló** (half a kilo), **dio/tria kilá** (two/three kilos), you can buy whatever quantity you want e.g. **misó kiló feta** (half a kilo of **feta**), **ena kiló domates** (a kilo of tomatoes), **enámiso kiló patates** (a kilo and a half of potatoes), **misó kiló kimá** (half a kilo of mincemeat), **tria/téssera kilá karpouzi** (three/four kilos of watermelon).

♦ **ti alo?** what else? It's important to understand this question.

♦ **aftá** that's all, nothing else. **Aftá** means literally 'these (things)' – the 'and nothing else' is understood.

Note: **o fournos** is literally 'an oven'; this is the colloquial word for a baker's. The sign on the shop will say **artopolion** or **artopiion**.

ena kiló = hília grammária

2 ♦ **thelo ena koutí spirta** I would like a box of matches (lit. I want one box matches). In Greek you don't put in the 'of' in phrases like these. (There is another example in dialogue 6.) A glass of water is **ena potiri neró** (lit. a glass water).

♦ **mikró i megalo** small or large. The endings of all adjectives are different in the masculine, feminine and neuter, e.g.

o mikrós kafés the small coffee	**o megalos stathmós** the large station
i mikrí karekla the small chair	**i megali tirópita** the large cheese pie
to mikró trapezi the small table	**to megalo karpouzi** the large watermelon

3 ♦ **éhete grammatósima?** do you have stamps?

yiá pou thelis? where do you want them for? (lit. for where do you want?). The man uses **thelis** (the familiar form) because he is speaking to a child.

yiá tin Anglia for England. Here are more examples: **yiá ti Gallia** (for France), **yiá tin Amerikí** (for America). Remember **i** becomes **ti(n)** after **apó** (from), **me** (with) and **yiá** (for).

ehi, pos there are, certainly. Here once again **ehi** (lit. he/she/it has) is used to mean 'there is/are'. Another example: **ehi psomí?** (is there any bread?), **pos, ehi** (certainly, there is).

doste mou ena give me one.

UNIT 7

4 *Anna is buying all sorts of things at the* **períptero**

Anna	Aftés tis dio kartes, parakaló.
Ipálilos	Ne, oriste. Típote alo?
Anna	Thelo ena periodikó ke ena miki maous.
Ipálilos	Ne, amesos.
Anna	Ke mia sokolata. Poso ine ola mazí?
Ipálilos	Ola mazí ine ekató drahmés.

i kartes postcards
to periodikó magazine
to miki maous Micky Mouse comic
i sokolata chocolate

5 *A tourist would like to buy stamps for England*

Tourístria	Mipos éhete grammatósima yiá Anglia?
Ipálilos	Ísos eho . . . ena leptó parakaló . . . posa thélete?
Tourístria	Dio.
Ipálilos	Oriste.

isos perhaps

4 ◆ **aftés tis dio kartes** these two postcards. **Aftés** is the plural of **aftí** which you learned in Unit 3. Note the word for 'these' changes with masculine, feminine and neuter nouns e.g.
aftí i andres these men
aftés i kartes these postcards
aftá ta grammatósima these stamps

◆ **típote alo** or **típota alo** anything else? **Típota** means both 'anything' and 'nothing'. On p. 82 you have **típota idiétero** (nothing special).

◆ **poso ine ola mazí?** how much is it altogether?

5 ◆ **mipos éhete . . .?** I wonder if you have . . . (see Unit 6, dialogue 1).

isos eho perhaps I have.

yiá Anglia for England.

◆ **posa?** how many? **Posa** is used with neuter nouns. **Posa grammatósima?** how many stamps?, **posa krevvatia?** how many beds?, **posa átoma?** how many people?

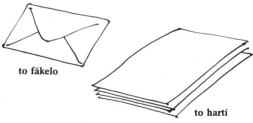

to fákelo

to hartí

6 *Buying cigarettes and matches*

Maria Thelo ena paketo amerikánika tsigara.
Vivi Oriste.
Maria Ke spirta parakaló.
Vivi Oriste, ine evdominda drahmés.
Maria Oriste, efharistó.

7 *Buying a toy car at a* **períptero**

Kiria Thelo ena aftokinitáki, parakaló.
Yiorgos Ne, pió? To aspro i to kítrino?
Kiria To kítrino, poso ine?
Yiorgos Evdominda pende drahmés mono.
Kiria Efharistó.
Yiorgos Parakaló.

8 *How about some racquets to play with on the beach?*

Pedí Kalimera kírie.
Kírios Kalimera.
Pedí Éhete rakétes?
Kírios Pos.
Pedí Ohi tou tennis.
Kírios Ohi.
Pedí Yiá ti thálassa.
Kírios Yiá ti thálassa.
Pedí Ti raketes éhete?
Kírios Orées, me plastikí laví. Diakoses eksinda drahmés.
Pedí Endaksi. Tha protimóusa to hroma prásino.

i raketes racquets
plastikí plastic
i laví handle

6   **ena paketo amerikánika tsigara** a pack of American cigarettes (lit. one pack American cigarettes). The adjective ends in **-a** to agree with the neuter noun **tsigaro**: **to amerikániko tsigaro** (the American cigarette), **ta amerikánika tsigara** (the American cigarettes).

7   **ena aftokinitaki** a little car. A car is **ena aftokínito** but as we saw in Unit 3, dialogue 7, you can make words diminutive by adding the ending **-aki** e.g. **pedí** (child), **pedaki** (little child), **psomí** (bread), **psomaki** (a roll).

pió? To aspro i to kítrino? which (one)? The white (one) or the yellow (one). Colors are adjectives. Here are three other colors:

♦ **o prásinos/kókkinos/mavros anaptiras** green/red/black lighter
i prásini/kókkini/mavri blouza green/red/black blouse
to prásino/kókkino/mavro kapelo green/red/black hat

♦ **mono** only. **Mono tin Kiriakí** (only on Sunday).

8   **ohi tou tennis** not for tennis (lit. not of the tennis).

♦ **yiá ti thálassa** for the beach (lit. for the sea).

ti raketes éhete? what sort of racquets do you have? (lit. what racquets do you have?). You might also need **ti psomí éhete?** (what sort of bread do you have?), **ti efimerides éhete?** (what sort of newspapers have you got?).

♦ **tha protimousa** I should prefer. It is easier and not impolite to use **protimó** (I prefer). You can see it written out in *Grammar* p. 101.

♦ **to hroma prásino** the green color (lit. the color green). You might hear the question: **ti hroma?** (what color?).

Key words and phrases

To learn

mipos éhete grammatósima?	I wonder do you have any stamps?
kartes?	post cards?
sokolata?	chocolate?
efimerides?	newspapers?

thelo ena mikró/megalo koutí	I'd like a small/large box
thelo ena kiló psomí	I'd like a kilo of bread
thelo misó kiló feta	I'd like half a kilo of feta
kimá	mincemeat
thelo dio kilá domates	I'd like two kilos of tomatoes
thelo tria kilà patates	I'd like three kilos of potatoes

aftá	that's all
poso ine ola mazí?	how much is it altogether?

típota	nothing/something
mono	only
yiá ti thálassa	for the beach (lit. for the sea)

protimó to mavro	I prefer the black (one)
kókkino	red (one)
aspro	white (one)
prásino	green (one)
kítrino	yellow (one)

eksakosa	600
eftakosa	700
oktakosa	800
eneakosa	900
hília	1000
dio hiliades	2,000

To understand

ti alo?	what else?
típota alo?	anything/something else
posa thélete?	how many do you want?
ti hroma?	what color?

Practice what you have learned

You should read the instructions to the following exercises before switching on the tape.

1 Complete the following conversation at a newsstand from the jumbled lines below. Check your answers with the tape.

Touristas Hérete.

Kiria Hérete.

Touristas *Éhete grammatósima yiá tin Anglía* (handwritten)

Kiria Ne, posa thélete?

Touristas *Tría parakaló* (handwritten)

Kiria Típota alo?

Touristas *Ne, ke aftés tis dio kartes* (handwritten)

Kiria Oriste.

Touristas *Poso ine ola mazí* (handwritten)

Kiria Ine eksinda tris drahmés

Touristas *Oriste, efharistó* (handwritten)

Kiria Parakaló.

Oriste, efharistó   Éhete grammatósima yiá tin Anglía?   poso ine ola mazí?   Ne, ke aftés tis dio kartes   Tria, parakaló

---

2 Here is a list of groceries bought at a small shop. Listen to the tape and write in the price of each item. (Answers p. 104)

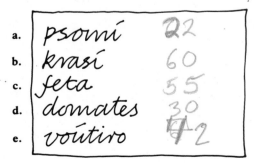

a. psomí   22
b. krasí   60
c. feta   55
d. domates 30
e. voútiro 42

UNIT 7

99

3 Listen to the tape, you will hear different words with colors, tick the correct color in your book. (Answers p. 104)

1
a. ☒ white
b. ☐ red
c. ☐ black

2
a. ☐ green
b. ☒ yellow
c. ☐ red

3
a. ☐ black
b. ☐ white
c. ☒ green

4
a. ☐ blue
b. ☐ black
c. ☒ red

5
a. ☒ red
b. ☐ blue
c. ☐ white

4 Complete the following conversation using **poso ine? prásino, tsigara, ekatón saranda dio, anaptira**. Listen to the tape and check your answers.

Petros Kalimera.

Dina Kalimera, thelo aftá ta .....*tsigara*.....................................

Petros Ne, oriste.

Dina Ke ena .....*anaptira*...

Petros Ti hroma?

Dina .....*prasina*...

Petros Típote alo?

Dina Ohi, ...*posi ine*............................. ola mazí?

Petros .....*eka*..................................drahmés

Dina Oriste.

Grammar

Adjectives

You have now come across a number of examples of how adjectives change their endings according to the nouns they are describing e.g. **o alos stathmós** (the other station), **ales dio tirópites** (another two cheese pies), **ta ala yévmata** (the other meals).

Adjectives usually precede the noun; however, if the adjective follows the noun – as it did, for example, in **avgá vrastá** (boiled eggs) – it is still clear from the endings that the words belong together. Here are a number of examples to show how adjectives change for masculine, feminine and neuter nouns in the singular and plural:

masculine **o kalós andras** the good man **i kalí andres** the good men
o ellinikós kafés the Greek coffee **i elliniki kafedes** the Greek coffees
o mikrós dromos the small road **i mikrí dromi** the small roads

feminine **i kalí yineka** the good woman **i kalés yinekes** the good women
i elliniki blouza the Greek blouse **i ellinikés blouzes** the Greek blouses
i mikrí karekla the small chair **i mikrés karekles** the small chairs

neuter **to kaló krasí** the good wine **ta kalá krasiá** the good wines
to ellinikó grammatósimo the Greek stamp **ta elliniká grammatósima** the Greek stamps
to mikró pedí the small child **ta mikrá pediá** the small children

Exercise Put the following nouns and adjectives into the plural and translate them into English. (Answers p. 104)

a. to kítrino aftokínito ....

b. i orea yineka ....

c. o mikrós stathmós ....

d. to alo pagotó ....

e. i mikrí adelfí ....

f. o ellinikós anaptiras ....

Protimó

The verb to note in this unit is **protimó** (I prefer)

protimó	I prefer	**protimame**	we prefer
protimás	you prefer	**protimate**	you prefer
protimá	he/she/it prefers	**protimane**	they prefer

kitó I look, **miló** I speak and **pernó** I pass all have the same endings.

The Greek alphabet

Letters you have already met

A α	'a' as in father		M μ	'm' as in my
B β	'v' as in van		Π π	'p' as in pie
Δ δ ς	'd' as in door		Σ σ ς	's' as in send
E ε	'e' as in let		T τ	't' as in tip
I ι	'i' as in police		Φ φ	'f ' as in four
K κ	'k' as in key		Ω ω	'o' as in hot

New letters

Letter	Name	Equivalent sound in English
N ν	ni	'n' as in never
P ρ	ro	'r' as in red

First cover the left-hand column and underline the new letters. Then uncover it and read the words out loud.

neró	νερό
enas	ἔνας
ne	ναί
parakaló	παρακαλώ
spirta	σπίρτα
prásino	πράσινο
minas	μίνας

Exercise Look at these signs, answer yes or no to the question and translate the word into English. The first one has been done for you. (Answers p. 104)

ΕΞΟΔΟΣ

Can you go out there? ...Yes....

a. ....Exit....

ΤΑΧΥΔΡΟΜΕΙΟ

Can you buy stamps here? ....

b. ....

O.T.E

Can you buy cigarettes here? ....

c. ....

ΠΛΗΡΟΦΟΡΙΕΣ

Can you get information here? ....

d. ....

ΣΤΑΣΙΣ

Can you buy stamps here? ....

e. ....

ΑΝΟΙΚΤΟ

Can you go into this shop? ....

f. ....

ΤΡΑΠΕΖΑ

Can you have a room here? ....

g. ....

ΞΕΝΟΔΟΧΕΙΟ

Can you sleep here? ....

h. ....

Did you know?

Shopping in Greece

Traditionally Greek shops open at 8:00 a.m. and close at about 2:00 p.m. for lunch and the siesta, and reopen around 5:00 p.m. for three or four hours. Some shops do not reopen in the evening on certain days and, except for some small groceries and bakeries, all shops are closed on Sunday. In recent years the state has attempted to 'Europeanize' shopping hours but has met with resistance from traders, so the only way of being sure is to ask or look at the times given in the window.

The bakery   ΑΡΤΟΠΩΛΕΙΟΝ   (artopolion/artopiion)

All bread is sold by weight (except rolls – **psomaki** – by item). Ordinary Greek bread is called **psomí**, which means both 'bread' and 'loaf', and is sold in kilo loaves; if you only want half ask for **misópsomi**. In towns you can also buy a French-style loaf, **frandzola** and brown bread, **mavropsomi** (lit. black bread). As many houses do not have ovens people bring their roasts to the baker to be cooked in his oven.

The pastry shop   ΖΑΧΑΡΟΠΛΑΣΤΕΙΟΝ   (zaharoplastion)

Apart from traditional Greek sweets like **baklava, katayifi** and **kourabiedes** (rich shortcake with almonds), pastry shops sell cakes and ice creams. There are also milk bars (**galaktopolion**) which sell milk products like ice cream, yogurt and rice puddings.

The butcher shop   ΚΡΕΟΠΩΛΕΙΟΝ   (kreopolion)

Butchers tend to keep most of their meat in the fridge – especially in summer – so don't be put off if the shop looks bare. You can expect to find **moshari** (beef), **hirinó** (pork), **kotópoulo** (chicken), **kimá** (mincemeat), **arní** (lamb) and sometimes **katsiki** (goat). Greek butchering techniques are somewhat haphazard so you will not find the same cuts as in other countries. Expect to pay the untrimmed weight of meat except when buying **bonfilé** (steak).

The newsstand   ΠΕΡΙΠΤΕΡΟ   (períptero)

There are newsstands everywhere you go in Greece and they provide an invaluable service selling cigarettes, newspapers, magazines, sweets, postcards, batteries, soap, contraceptives, books, stamps – in fact, almost anything you can think of. Most of them have telephones for public use and some sell cold drinks and ice cream.

The notions store   ΨΙΛΙΚΑ   (psiliká)

These little shops sell very much the same things as newsstands but also have larger toys and sewing items like buttons, thread and ribbons.

Your turn to speak

Read the introduction to each exercise and then work with the tape alone. You are going to practice asking for postcards, stamps etc. at the **períptero** (newsstand).

1 You are at the **períptero** in **Platia Syntagmatos**. You want to buy some stamps, postcards and a magazine. Use **thelo** (I would like) and **éhete?** (have you?). Then **poso ine ola mazi** (how much is it altogether?).

2 Now you're about to go onto the beach. You need some racquets. You're going to ask for big red racquets using **megales** and **kókkines**.

Answers

Practice what you have learned p. 99 Exercise **2** (**a**) 22 (**b**) 60 (**c**) 55 (**d**) 30 (**e**) 42.

p. 100 Exercise **3** 1a, 2b, 3c, 4c, 5a.

Grammar p. 101 (**a**) ta kítrina aftokínita, the yellow cars (**b**) i orées yinekes, the beautiful women (**c**) i mikrí stathmí, the small stations (**d**) ta ala pagotá, the other ice-creams (**e**) i mikrés adelfés, the little sisters (**f**) i ellinikí anaptires, the Greek lighters.

The Greek alphabet p. 102 (**a**) yes, exit (**b**) yes, Post Office (**c**) no, the Telecommunications Organization of Greece (**d**) yes, Information (**e**) no, Bus stop (**f**) yes, Open (**g**) no, Bank (**h**) yes, Hotel.

8 Shopping – Part 2

You will learn

- to ask for things in the pharmacy
- to ask for groceries
- to ask for vegetables at the market
- to buy clothes
- to make comparisons
- to understand polite apologies

Study guide

	Dialogues 1–3: listen without the book
	Dialogues 1–3: listen, read and study one by one
	Dialogues 4–6: listen without the book
	Dialogues 4–6: listen, read and study one by one
	Dialogues 7, 8: listen without the book
	Dialogues 7, 8: listen, read and study one by one
	Study *Key words and phrases*
	Complete the exercises in *Practice what you have learned*
	Study *Grammar* and do the exercise
	Do *The Greek alphabet* and complete the exercise
	Read *Did you know?*
	Do the taped exercises in *Your turn to speak*
	Finally, listen to all the dialogues again.

Dialogues

1 At the pharmacy

Sofia	Kalimera.
Farmakopiós	Kalimera, ti thélete parakaló?
Sofia	Ena koutí aspirines.
Farmakopiós	Ena megalo koutí i ena mikró?
Sofia	Ena mikró.
Farmakopiós	Ne, efharístos . . . misó leftó na to tilikso.

i/o farmakopiós pharmacist (person)

2 Yiannis wants to buy some toothpaste

Yiannis	Mia odondókrema 'Binaka', parakaló.
Farmakopiós	Ti alo?
Yiannis	Aftá. Ah! . . . ne . . . ke . . . mia . . . pos to lene? Vourtsa yiá ta dóndia.
Farmakopiós	Ti hroma?
Yiannis	O ti nane.

i odondókrema toothpaste
i vourtsa brush
ta dóndia teeth

3 Kiria Irini is buying buttons but can't find the right size

Kírios Diamantis	Madám, lipoume . . . den ehi mikró.
Kiria Irini	Den ehi, eh?
Kírios Diamantis	Den eho mikrá. . . Ah! tiherí iste.
Kiria Irini	Tétio . . . alá se pió. . .
Kírios Diamantis	Ne, pió mikró, to blé.

madám madam
lipoume I'm sorry
tétio such, similar
alá but
ble blue

1 ♦ **ti thélete, parakaló?** what would you like please?

ena koutí (aspirines) a box of (aspirins). You have learned how to ask using **thelo** (I would like) e.g. **thelo ena koutí spirta** (I would like a box of matches), but you can omit the verb and just name the object you want to buy e.g. **dio grammatósima yiá Anglia** (two stamps for England), **tris kartes** (three postcards), **ena paketo amerikánika tsigara** (a pack of American cigarettes).

♦ **ena megalo koutí i ena mikró?** a large box or a small (one)?
Remember that adjectives usually precede the nouns they are describing (see p. 101). The **i** here means 'or'.

misó leftó . . . na to tilikso just a minute . . . let me wrap it up (lit. **miso leftó** half a minute).

2 ♦ **pos to lene?** what's it called? (lit. what do they call it?). A useful little phrase to give you time to think e.g. **ena boukali . . . pos to lene? ouzo** (a bottle . . . what's it called? ouzo), **ena . . . pos to lene? psomí** (one . . . what's it called? bread).

♦ **o ti nane** it doesn't matter which (lit. whatever).

dóndia
teeth

odondoyiatrós   **odondóponos**
dentist   toothache

3 ♦ **madám, lipoume** madam, I'm sorry/afraid. **Lipoume** is a polite way of expressing regrets e.g. **lipoume, den boró . . .** (I'm sorry, I can't . . .) **den ehi mikró** (there isn't a small one).

tiherí iste you are lucky. **Tiherí** has the ending for a woman; if it referred to a man it would be **tiherós**. We have already seen **kourasmenos/ kourasmeni** (tired) and **pandremenos/pandremeni** (married).

♦ **pió mikró** smaller (lit. more small). **Pió** is used to make comparisons; it is very easy to use since it always remains in the same form and does not change according to gender e.g. **pió megali** bigger (f.), **pió megalo** bigger (n.). The *Grammar* section of this unit is about comparisons made with **pió**.

4 *At the open market*

Enas Kírios	Thelo na mou dosis ena kiló eliés . . . ehis?
Ipálilos	Eho, eho.
Enas Kírios	Poso ehi to kiló?
Ipálilos	Evdominda dio.
Enas kírios	I ksidates?
Ipálilos	I ksidates éhoune eneninda.
Enas Kírios	Orées i ksidates . . .
Ipálilos	Orées.
Enas Kírios	Boró na dokimaso?
Ipálilos	Borite, eléfthera kírie.

i eliés olives
ksidates pickled

5 *In a grocery. What does it all cost?*

Bakalis	Amesos, éhoume ta avgá, íkosi pende, éhoume ena kiló záhari, ikositrís ke peninda, éhoume . . . edó ti ine? Rizi?
Vaso	Ne.
Bakalis	Rizi. To rizi, peninda drahmés. Ah! . . . éhoume ke meli. To meli ena koutaki? Saranda tris ke peninda. Ola mazí? Pende . . . deka . . . téssera . . . eptá . . . ke pende . . . dódeka . . . pende . . . deka . . . dódeka . . . ke dio dekatéssera. Málista despinís mou, ola mazí ine ekatón saranda dio drahmés.
Vaso	Efharistó.

o bakalis grocer
i záhari sugar
to rizi rice
to koutaki small box/pot

4 ♦ **thelo na mou dosis** I'd like you to give me. This is the familiar form you could use with a shopkeeper you know well. You should normally use **thelo na mou dósete**. Here are some more examples: **thelo na mou dósete ena kiló eliés** (I'd like you to give me a kilo of olives), **thelo na mou dósete dio litra gala** (I'd like you to give me two liters of milk), **thelo na mou dósete misó kiló kimá** (I'd like you to give me half a kilo of mincemeat).

poso ehi to kiló? how much is a kilo? (lit. how much has the kilo?)

♦ **boró na dokimaso?** can I taste? **Na dokimaso** can also be used if you want to try on clothes, e.g. **boró na dokimaso aftó to fórema?** (can I try on this dress?), **boró na dokimaso aftés tis eliés?** (can I taste these olives?). Do you remember **na** in phrases such as: **boró na alakso?** (can I change?) This is another example of how **na** is used to link two verbs.

eléfthera go ahead (lit. freely). Remember **eléfthera** was used in this phrase **ine eléftheri aftí i karekla?** (is this chair free?).

5 ♦ **edó, ti ine?** here, what is it? You could say here **aftó, ti ine?** what is this? The reply would be **aftó ine ouzo/krasí/meli** (this is ouzo/wine/honey etc.).

éhoume ke meli we've got honey, too. Yet another example of **ke** meaning 'too/as well' as in **k'egó** (me too).

6 *Eleni is giving the grocer's son a list of things to be delivered*

Eleni   Lipón . . . tha íthela na mou stílete, dio boukália ladi.
Pedí   Ne.
Eleni   Ena kiló záhari.
Pedí   Ne.
Eleni   Ligo kafé.
Pedí   Ne.
Eleni   Um . . . deka avgá.
Pedí   Ne.
Eleni   Metá thelo ligo . . . ti alo na paro . . . ti mou lipi? Ah! tha mou stílete eksi koka koles litroú . . . tha mou stílete dio krasiá ke merikés, um, marmelades.
Pedí   Ne. Poses?
Eleni   Na mou stílete mia veríkoko, mia damáskino ke mia pikró portokali.

to boukali bottle
to ladi oil
metá after
litroú litre (size)
to veríkoko apricot
to damáskino plum
pikrós-i-o bitter
to portokali orange

7 *Lakis is shopping in Monastiraki for a Greek embroidered dress for his girlfriend*

Lakis   Thelo ena fórema ellinikís tehnis.
Ipálilos   Ti méyethos parakaló?
Lakis   Saranda eksi.
Ipálilos   Sas aresi aftó?
Lakis   Ne, polí oreo. Poso ine?
Ipálilos   Hílies drahmés.
Lakis   Oriste.
Ipálilos   Efharistó.

to fórema dress
ellinikos-i-o Greek
tehnis craft
méyethos size

8 *Maria wants to buy an embroidered blouse*

Maria   Éhete vamvákeres blouzes?
Viky   Ne, éhoume.
Maria   Thelo mia aspri, saranda dio noúmero me kókkino kéndima.
Viky   Oriste.
Maria   Ah! ine polí orea, poso tin éhete?
Viky   Dio hiliades.
Maria   Polí akriví ine. Efharistó.

aspros-i-o white

6 **tha íthela na mou stílete** I'd like you to send me (see p. 129 for **mou**).

ligo kafé a little coffee. Some other examples: **liyi záhari** (a little sugar), **ligo rizi** (a little rice), **liyi feta** (a little **feta**, Greek white cheese).

metá after.

◆ **ti alo na paro?** what else do I need? (lit. what else should I take?). Do you remember **ti alo?** (what else?).

ti mou lipi? what haven't I got? (lit. what is lacking to me). Here is another useful phrase to give you time to think.

tha mou stílete would you send me (lit. you'll send me).

merikés (marmelades) some (jam). This word **merikés** has to agree with the next word e.g. **merikí andres** (some men), **merikés yinekes** (some women), **meriká pediá** (some children), **meriká portokália** (some oranges), **merikés domates** (some tomatoes), **meriká mila** (some apples), **merikés patates** (some potatoes).

7 **ellinikís tehnis** Greek craft (traditionally embroidered). **Tehnis** can sometimes mean 'art' in a general way or a craft trade.

◆ **ti méyethos?** what size? If you don't know your size and you want to try it on you can say: **boró na dokimaso?**

sas aresi aftó? do you like this? (lit. it pleases you this?). 'I like it' is **mou aresi aftó** (lit. it pleases me this).

◆ **polí oreo** very beautiful. This phrase is very common in Greek.

8 ◆ **éhete vamvákeres blouzes?** do you have cotton blouses? 'A shirt' is **ena poukámiso** and 'a pair of trousers' **ena pandeloni**.

thelo mia aspri I want a white (one).

saranda dio noúmero size 42 (lit. 42 number).

me kókkino kéndima with red embroidery.

poso tin éhete? how much is it? (lit. how much do you have it?).

◆ **polí akriví ine** it is very expensive. Here are some more examples with **akrivós** (expensive) and **ftinós** (cheap):

o akrivós/ftinós kafés	the expensive/cheap coffee
i akriví/ftiní fousta	the expensive/cheap skirt
to akrivó/ftinó fórema	the expensive/cheap dress

UNIT 8

Key words and phrases

To learn

thelo ena koutí aspirines	I'd like a box of aspirins
thelo mia odondókrema	I'd like a tube of toothpaste
mia vourtsa yiá ta dóndia	toothbrush
na mou dósete ena kiló	would you give me one kilo of
eliés	olives
rizi	rice
záhari	sugar
na mou dósete	would you give me
ena litro ladi	one litre of oil
dio litra gala	two litres of milk
thelo ena fórema	I'd like a dress
mia fousta	a skirt
mia blouza	a blouse
ena poukámiso	a shirt
ena pandeloni	a pair of trousers
pió mikró	smaller
pió megalo	bigger
boró na dokimaso	may I try/taste it
ti alo na paro?	what else should I take?
o ti nane	it doesn't matter which
ine polí akrivó	it's very expensive
ftinó	cheap
polí oreo	very beautiful/nice

To understand

ti thélete, parakaló?	what would you like, please?
ti méyethos?	what size?
ena megalo i ena mikró?	a large or a small?
lipoume	I'm sorry

Practice what you have learned

Before beginning each exercise read the instructions, then play the tape and write your answers in the spaces provided.

1 Sofia does some shopping at the **bakáliko** (grocery). Listen to the tape and make a list of what she buys and how much she spends. (Answers p. 118)

bouka ladi	*55*
2 mar	*62*
Kati cafe	*35*
kilo olies	*40*
10 avga	*36*
Total	*268*

2 The following dialogue is only half complete. Listen to the tape and fill in Vaso's part from the jumbled sentences below.

Ipálilos   Kalimera, ti thélete, parakaló?

Vaso   *thelo ena kouti meli*

Ipálilos   Amesos, ti alo?

Vaso   *ena kiló zahari*

Ipálilos   Ne, ena kiló.

Vaso   *ena boukali ladi*

Ipálilos   Ena megalo boukali i ine mikró?

Vaso   *ena mikro*

Ipálilos   Típote alo?

Vaso   *ke eksi avga. Afta pose ine?*

Ipálilos   Amesos, ena koutí meli, saranda dio drahmés; ena kiló záhari, peninda eftá; ena boukali ladi, trianda tris; eksi avgá íkosi drahmés. Ola mazí: ekatón peninda dio drahmés.

Vaso   *oriste*

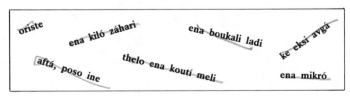

oriste
ena kiló záhari
ena boukali ladi
ke eksi avgá
aftá, poso ine
thelo ena koutí meli
ena mikró

3 Listen to the tape and tick the things Anna buys and note the weight. (Answers p. 118).

☑ eliés   *miso kilo*

☑ patates   *3 kilo*

☑ psomí   *1 kilo*

☑ domates   *2 kila*

☐ kimá   *miso kilo*

☐ kafés

☐ záhari

☐ avgá

☐ krasí

☐ karpouzi *6 kilo*

4 The words in the first line of each of these dialogues are jumbled up. Put the words in order with the help of the tape, then translate them into English. (Answers p. 118)

a. koutí thelo aspirínes ena Ne, amesos

....

b. íne poso mazí ola? Ekatón saranda drahmés, ola mazí

....

....

c. na boró dokimáso to? Ne, boríte

....

....

Grammar

Making comparisons

As you saw in dialogue 3 of this unit, you can make comparisons by putting the word **pió** (more) in front of adjectives e.g.

pió mikró smaller	**pió ftinó** cheaper
pió megalo bigger	**pió akrivó** more expensive

You can also use **pió** with adverbs e.g.

pió sigá more slowly	**pió kalá** better
pió grígora more quickly	**pió argá** later

If you want to form a superlative – best, worst, smallest, biggest etc. – you simply put the word for 'the' (**o**, **i** or **to**) in front of the **pió** e.g.

aftós o andras ine pió megalos	this man is bigger
aftós o andras ine o pió megalos	this man is the biggest
aftí i fousta ine pió ftiní	this skirt is cheaper
aftí i fousta ine i pió ftiní	this skirt is the cheapest
aftó to krasí ine pió kaló	this wine is better
aftó to krasí ine to pió kaló	this wine is the best

If you want to say 'more' by itself use **pió polí** e.g. **thélete pió polí?** do you want (some) more?, **efharistó, de thelo pió polí** thank you, I don't want (any) more. 'Enough!' is **ftani!**

Exercise

Translate these sentences into English. (Answers p. 118)

a. Aftó to krasí ine to pió akrivó ....

b. Thelo mia fousta pió ftiní ....

c. Aftó to ouzo ine to pió ftinó ....

d. Aftó to karpouzi ine to pió megalo ....

e. Aftí i eliá ine i pió mikrí ....

f. Thelo ena domátio pió megalo ....

g. O ellinikós kafés ine polí kalós ....

h. Aftó to portokali ine to pió mikró ....

i. Aftó to voútiro den ine to pió ftinó ....

j. Aftó to aftokínito ine to pió akrivó ....

Dino

The verb to note in this unit is **dino** (I give)

dino	I give	**dínoume**	we give
dinis	you give	**dínete**	you give
dini	he/she/it gives	**dínoune**	they give

The Greek alphabet

Letters you have already met

A α	'a' as in father	N ν	'n' as in never
B β	'v' as in van	Π π	'p' as in pie
Δ δ	'd' as in door	P ρ	'r' as in red
E ε	'e' as in let	Σ σ ς	's' as in send
I ι	'i' as in police	T τ	't' as in tip
K κ	'k' as in key	Φ φ	'f' as in four
M μ	'm' as in my	Ω ω	'o' as in hot

New letters

Letter	Name	Equivalent sound in English
O o	ómikron	'o' as in hot
Λ λ	lamda	'l' as in live

Exercise Read through Sofia's shopping list (Answers p. 118)

1 This is a shopping list for the
a. ☐ farmakio
b. ☐ tahidromio
c. ☐ bakáliko

2 How many kilos of tomatoes does she buy?
a. ☐ half a kilo
b. ☐ a kilo
c. ☐ two kilos

3 Does she buy?
a. ☐ a large bag of coffee
b. ☐ a small bag of coffee
c. ☐ a small bag of tea

4 Does she buy meat?
a. ☐ yes
b. ☐ no

5 Does she buy?
a. ☐ three kilos of potatoes
b. ☐ two kilos of potatoes
c. ☐ a kilo of potatoes

"Ένα κιλό ντομάτες
μισό κιλό ελιές
τρία κιλά πατάτες
μισό κιλό φέτα
ένα ἄσπρο κρασί
"ένα μικρό κουτί
καφέ

Did you know?

The pharmacy

Pharmacies generally follow the opening hours of other shops. If you find one closed there will be a list of druggists on duty in the window. Certain pharmacists take turns staying open all night – the others display illuminated lists of all-night drugstores ΔΙΑΝΥΚΤΕΡΕΥΟΝΤΑ ΦΑΡΜΑΚΕΙΑ (**dianikterévonta farmakia**). Many druggists offer advice on minor complaints (and even examine their customers!) and most medicines can be bought without a prescription.

Monastiraki

Shopping in Athens and Thessaloniki

Although you will see many imported products in the shops, Greece has made great strides in recent years in the manufacture of goods at home. For example, it is now possible to buy a very wide range of stylish and well-made Greek clothes and shoes. In Thessaloniki there is a large shopping district in the wide streets behind the waterfront and prices are, on the whole, lower than in the capital. In Athens most of the best clothing and shoe shops are on the streets which run into Syntagma Square: Ermou, Voukarestiou, Stadiou and Panepistimiou. The most expensive and exclusive shops are around Kolonaki Square. Below the Akropolis there is a street which runs through the square of Monastiraki. At the upper end there are shops selling souvenirs, antiques and Greek handicrafts (**ellinikís tehnis**). After the square the street becomes a flea market where you can buy secondhand clothes, books, furniture and so on. In both the tourist shops and in the market even if prices are marked you stand a good chance of getting the price down if you haggle.

The grocer

Apart from the usual food and drink most grocers stock a wide range of household goods including lightbulbs, bottled gas etc. In the larger ones you collect bills at the different counters and pay at a central check-out counter.

What size are you?

Ladies' dresses, etc.		
	U.S.	Gr
	10	38
	12	40
foustes	14	42
forémata	16	44
paltá	18	46
	20	48
	22	50

Men's shirts		
	U.S.	Gr
	14	36
	14½	37
	15	38
poukámisa	15½	39
	16	40
	16½	41

Shoes		
	U.S.	Gr
	6	37
	6½	38
	7½	39
	8	40
papoútsia	8½	41
	9½	42
	10½	43
	11½	44

Men's suits		
	U.S.	Gr
	36	46
	38	48
koustoúmia	40	50
	42	52
	44	54

Your turn to speak

1 You are in a small shop in Monastiraki and you want to buy a white dress, but the one you choose is very big (**megalo**), you'd like a smaller one (**pió mikró**) but that's yellow (**kítrino**) and very expensive (**polí akrivó**).

2 You are in a **bakáliko**; you are going to buy **eliés** (olives) **psomí** (bread) and **liyi feta** (a little feta cheese).

Answers

Practice what you have learned p. 113 Exercise **1** ena boukali ladi (55), dio marmelades (62), ena koutí kafé (35), misó kiló eliés (40), deka avgá (36). Total 228 drahmes.

p. 114 Exercise **3** eliés (½ kilo), patates (3 kilá), psomí (1 kilo), domates (2 kilá), kimá (½ kilo), karpouzi (6 kilos).

p. 114 Exercise **4 (a)** thelo ena koutí aspirines, I want a box of aspirins **(b)** poso ine ola mazí? how much is it altogether? **(c)** boró na to dokimaso? may I try it?

Grammar p. 115 **(a)** This wine is the most expensive **(b)** I want a cheaper skirt **(c)** This ouzo is the cheapest **(d)** This watermelon is bigger **(e)** This olive is the smallest **(f)** I want a bigger room **(g)** Greek coffee is very good **(h)** This orange is the smallest **(i)** This butter is not the cheapest **(j)** This car is the most expensive.

The Greek alphabet p. 116 1c, 2b, 3b, 4b, 5a.

9 Making travel arrangements

You will learn

- to buy tickets for bus and train trips
- to arrange excursions
- to rent a car
- to ask for service at a garage
- to ask about distances

Before you begin

You are going to learn about travelling around in Greece. By now some of the general ways of asking should be familiar to you so you should concentrate on the phrases specifically related to travel. Follow the pattern in the *Study guide* remembering to tick each section as you complete it.

Study guide

	Dialogues 1–3: listen without the book
	Dialogues 1–3: listen, read and study one by one
	Dialogues 4, 5: listen without the book
	Dialogues 4, 5: listen, read and study one by one
	Dialogues 6–8: listen without the book
	Dialogues 6–8: listen, read and study one by one
	Study *Key words and phrases*
	Complete the exercises in *Practice what you have learned*
	Study *Grammar* and do the exercise
	Do *The Greek alphabet* and complete the exercise
	Read *Did you know?*
	Do the taped exercises in *Your turn to speak*
	Listen to all the dialogues again.
	Finally, do *Revision/Review Units 7–9* at the end of the book

Dialogues

1 Taking a taxi

Odigós Pou tha pate, parakaló?
Eleni Stin Omonia.
Odigós Stin Omonia se pió simio akrivós?
Sofia Sto ksenodohio Amarilys.
Eleni Poso ine, parakaló?
Odigós Dio leptá na stamatiso.

o odigós driver
to simio place

2 Renting a car

Kírios Kalispera sas.
Ipálilos Kalispera sas.
Kírios Thelo na enikiaso ena aftokínito.
Ipálilos Ti aftokínito protimate?
Kírios Ena 'Fiat'.
Ipálilos Yiá poso keró to thélete?
Kírios Peripou deka meres.
Ipálilos Boró na do tin ádia odiyiseós sas.
Kírios Ne. Oriste.

peripou about
i ádia odiyíseos driver's license

3 At the railway station

Kírios Parakaló, ena isitírio yiá ti Larisa.
Ipálilos Ti thesi parakaló?
Kírios Proti.
Ipálilos Apló i me epistrofí?
Kírios Apló. Poso ine?
Ipálilos Pendakoses drahmés.
Kírios Efharistó.
Ipálilos Parakaló.

to isitírio ticket
i thesis seat, place, class
proti first
apló one-way (lit. simple)

1   **pou tha pate?** where to? (lit. where will you go?). **Pao** (I go) is written out in full in *Grammar*, Unit 5.

stin Omonia to Omonia (Square).

se pió simio akrivós? to which place precisely? You came across **akrivós** meaning 'precisely, exactly' in *Grammar*, Unit 6.

dió leptá just a minute (lit. two minutes).

na stamatiso let me stop. This use of **na** is as in **na sas sistiso**. . . (may I introduce. . .) and **na pame** (let's go).

2 ◆ **thelo na enikiaso**   I'd like to rent.

◆ **ti aftokínito protimate?** which car do you prefer? **Protimó** (I prefer) is set out in *Grammar*, Unit 7. Some other examples:
ti protimate kafé i tsai? which do you prefer tea or coffee?
ti protimate aspro i kókkino krasí? which do you prefer white or red wine?

◆ **yiá poso keró to thélete?** for how long do you want it? You could say:
yiá poses meres? (for how many days?).

◆ **boró na do?** can/may I see?

3 ◆ **ena isitírio yiá ti Larisa** a ticket for Larisa. If you need more than one ticket: **dio/tria/téssera isitíria** (two/three/four tickets).

◆ **apló i me epistrofí?** one-way or round-trip? (lit. one-way or with return?).

4 *Dimitris wants to know if there is a restaurant on the boat*

Dimitris Iparhi estiatório sto plio?
Ipálilos Ohi, s'aftá ta ferry boat den iparhi estiatório mesa, alá iparhi bar, ke borite na párete kafé, anapsiktiká, sandwich, tétia prámata.
Dimitris Efharistó polí.

ta anapsiktiká refreshments

5 *Booking an excursion at the tourist agency*

Kiria Anna Thelo na kliso tris thesis yiá mia ekdromí.
Ipálilos Ne endaksi, yiá pou?
Kiria Anna Yiá to Nafplio.
Ipálilos Ne, oriste.
Kiria Anna Poso ine, parakaló?
Ipálilos Hílies pendakoses drahmés to átomo.
Kiria Anna Toso akrivó?
Ipálilos Ma, ine me fayitó.
Kiria Anna Tote, endaksi.

i ekdromí excursion
ma but
tote then

6 *Getting gasoline and a tire changed*

Kiria Anna Parakaló, íkosi litra venzini.
Ipálilos Ne, super i aplí?
Kiria Anna Super.
Ipálilos Amesos.
Kiria Anna Borite na mou aláksete to lástiho.
Ipálilos Ne, efharistos.
Kiria Anna Efharistó.

ta litra liters
i venzini gasoline
to lástiho tire

4 ♦ **iparhi estiatório sto plio?** is there a restaurant on the boat?

den iparhi estiatório (mesa), alá iparhi bar there isn't a restaurant (inside), but there's a bar.

borite na párete you can get (lit. you can take).

♦ **tétia prámata** things like that (lit. such things). The word for 'thing' is **prama**; like other neuter nouns ending in -a, the plural is made by adding -ta e.g. **fórema, forémata** (dresses), and **kima, kímata** (waves).

5 ♦ **thelo na kliso tris thesis** I'd like to book three places (lit. I want to close. . .).

♦ **to átomo** per person (lit. the person).

♦ **toso akrivó** so expensive? The word **toso** (so) changes with the gender of the noun it's describing. Here it is with the adjectives in the masculine, feminine and neuter: **tosos kalós** (so good), **tosi ftiní** (so cheap), **toso polí** (so much).

me fayitó with food. **Fayitó** means both 'food' and 'a meal' e.g. **ena oreo fayitó** a delicious meal.

6 ♦ **super i aplí?** super or regular? (lit. super or simple). Small cars can run on regular but you would be wiser to put in super.

♦ **borite na (mou) aláksete to lástiho?** can you change the tire (for me)? The two verbs are linked again by **na** and are both in the 'you' form. For other uses of **mou**, see *Grammar* in this unit.

7 *At the garage*

Dimitris Endaksi, ta ládia. . . Ah! orea, edó ine. I deksamení ine yemati. Típota alo thélete parakaló?
Kírios Ohi, efharistó. Poso prepi ne pliroso?
Dimitris Dio hiliades pendakoses eksinda.
Kírios Efharistó.

ta ládia oil

to kapó
to paráthiro
ta fanária
i porta
to lástiho

8 *How far is it between Athens and Kifissia?*

Sofia Posa hiliómetra ine i Kifissia apó tin Athina?
Kírios I Kifissia, stin Platia Kifissias ine yiro sta dódeka hiliómetra.

ta hiliómetra kilometre
i platia square

7 ◆ **i deksamení ine yemati** the tank is full. The adjective **yematos** (full) changes its ending like other adjectives e.g. **o stathmós ine yematos** (the station is full), **i valitsa ine yemati** (the suitcase is full), **to ksenodohio ine yemato** (the hotel is full). Empty is **ádios**.

típota alo thélete? do you want anything else? Greek word order is very flexible: the order could be **thélete típota alo** without changing the meaning.

poso prepi na pliroso? how much have I to pay?

8 ◆ **posa hiliómetra ine i Kifissia apó tin Athina?** how many kilometres is it from Kifissia to Athens? Note that both the place names are feminine and so have the feminine form of 'the' – **i** in front of them (the second **i** has changed to **ti(n)** because it follows **apó**). Other ways of asking how far/how long will it take? : **ine kondá?** (is it near?), **ine makriá?** (is it far?), **posa leptá?** (how many minutes?), **poses ores?** (how many hours?).

Platia Kifissias Kifissia Square.

◆ **yiro sta dodeka hiliómetra** about twelve kilometres. Other examples: **yiro stis enea i ora** (about nine o'clock), **yiro sti mia** (about one).

Key words and phrases

To learn

thelo na enikiaso ena aftokínito	I'd like to rent a car
poso ine tin imera?	how much is it a day?
to hiliómetro?	a kilometer?
ena isitírio yiá . . .	one ticket for. . .
ena isitírio yiá. . . me epistrofí	one round-trip ticket for. . .
dio/tria isitíria yiá. . .	two/three tickets for. . .
thelo na kliso thesis yiá. . .	I want to reserve seats for. . .
mia ekdromí	an excursion
toso akrivó?	so expensive?
iparhi estiatório sto plio?	is there a restaurant on the boat?
iparhoun toualetes sto treno?	are there toilets on the train?
íkosi litra venzini	20 liters of gasoline
borite na mou aláksete to lástiho?	can you change the tire for me?
posa hiliómetra ine?	how many kilometers is it?
ine makriá?	is it far?
ine kondá?	is it near?
poses ores ine apó. . .?	how many hours is it from. . .?

To understand

pou pate?	where are you going?
pou akrivós?	where exactly?
ti protimate?	what do you prefer?
yiá poses meres?	for how many days?
yiá pou?	for where?
apló i me epistrofí?	one-way or round-trip?
super i aplí?	super or regular?
tétia prámata	things like that
to átomo	per person
yiro	around, about
boró na do tin ádia odiyíseós sas?	may I see your driver's license?
i deksamení ine yemati	the tank is full

Practice what you have learned

You should read the instructions to each exercise before switching on the tape.

1 You will hear three short conversations at the ticket office. Listen to each one and enter the destination, number of passengers and the total fare in the table below. **Pros** to, towards, **átoma** people, **timí** price. (Answers p. 132)

		Pros	Átoma	Timí
1	Apó Athina			
2	Apó Athina			
3	Apó Athina			

2 Listen to the tape and tick the things Anna asks for at the garage. (Answers p. 132)

a. ☐ Íkosi litra venzini super

b. ☐ Deka litra super

c. ☐ Borite na aláksete to lástiho?

d. ☐ Borite na aláksete ta ládia?

e. ☐ Ke ta ládia

f. ☐ Ke to lástiho

g. ☐ Ke to neró

h. ☐ Thelo neró

3 Listen to the tape and complete the following conversation choosing the appropriate phrase.

Odigós   Pou pate parakaló?
Tourístria Stin Platia Sintagmatos/stin Platia Omonias
Odigós   Se pió simio akrivós?
Tourístria Stin taverna/stin Ethnikí Trápeza
Odigós   Ah! katálava, apó pou iste?
Tourístria Apó ti Gallia/apó tin Anglia
Odigós   Edó ine i trapeza.
Tourístria Poso ine?/poso ine ola mazí?
Odigós   Ekatón peninda drahmés.
Tourístria Oriste/efharistó.

4 Yiannis wants to hire a car, but his part of the conversation is incomplete. The missing sentences are below. Complete the dialogue and listen to the tape to check your answers.

Yiannis ....

Vaso   Boró na do tin ádia odiyiseós sas?

Yiannis ....

Vaso   Ti aftokínito protimate?

Yiannis ....

Vaso   Ena Fiat 127?

Yiannis ....

Vaso   Tetrakoses saranda tin iméra ke enea drahmés to hiliómetro.

Yiannis ....

Vaso   Yiá poses meres to thélete?

Yiannis ....

Vaso   Endaksi.

ne oriste

thelo na enikiaso ena aftokínito

yiá pende meres

mália poso ine?

endaksi

ena Fiat alá ohi polí mikró

Grammar

Expressing possession

Do you remember **pió ine to onomá sas?** (what is your name?) and **aftós ine o andras mou** (this is my husband)? In these examples **sas** (your) and **mou** (my) express possession. Here is a list of all the words of this type you will need:

mou	my	**mas**	our
sou	your (familiar)	**sas**	your (polite and plural)
tou/tis/tou	his/hers/its	**tous**	their

All these words *follow* the noun e.g.

o kafés mou my coffee (lit. the coffee of me)
o andras tis her husband (lit. the husband of her)
i valitsa tou his suitcase (lit. the suitcase of him)
to diavatirió sas your passport (lit. the passport of you)

Note that you still put 'the' in front of the nouns. All these words are also used to mean 'to me', 'to you', 'to him' etc.

doste mou ena boukali krasí give me a bottle of wine (lit. give to me a bottle of wine)
mas lene they tell us (lit. to us they tell)
tis dini he gives her (lit. to her he gives)

Exercise

Translate these sentences into English. (Answers p. 132)

a. Thelo to diavatirió sas ....

b. Pou ine to ksenodohio sas? ....

c. Aftó ine to aftokinitó mas ....

d. Aftí ine i valitsa mou ....

e. Théloume to proinó mas ....

f. Doste mou ta diavatiriá sas ....

g. I karekla tis ine eléftheri ....

h. To domátio mou ine edó ....

Klino

The verb to note in this unit is **klino** (I close, shut)

klino	I close	**klínoume**	we close
klinis	you close	**klínete**	you close
klini	he/she/it closes	**klínoune**	they close

Don't forget the expressions **klino mia thesi** (I book a seat/place), **klínoume dio thesis** (we book two seats/places).

The Greek alphabet

Letters you have already met

A α	'a' as in father		N ν	'n' as in never
B β	'v' as in van		O o	'o' as in hot
Δ δ	'd' as in door		Π π	'p' as in pie
E ε	'e' as in let		P ρ	'r' as in red
I ι	'i' as in police		Σ σ ς	's' as in send
K κ	'k' as in key		T τ	't' as in tip
Λ λ	'l' as in live		Φ φ	'f' as in four
M μ	'm' as in my		Ω ω	'o' as in hot

New letters

Letter	Name	Equivalent sound in English
Θ θ	thita	'th' as in this
Γ γ	gama	'g' as in guild 'y' as in yet (before 'e' and 'i')

First cover the left-hand column and underline the new letters. Then uncover it and read the words out loud.

thelo	θέλω
thálassa	θάλασσα
kathe	κάθε
gala	γάλα
yiá	γιά
yiatí	γιατί
galliká	γαλλικά
grammatósimo	γραμμάτοσιμο
Yiorgios	Γεώργιος
thesi	θέση
Thessaloniki	Θεσσαλονίκη

Exercise   Can you identify these towns and cities? (Answers p. 132)

a. ΘΕΣΣΑΛΟΝΙΚΗ ....

b. ΑΘΗΝΑ ....

c. ΠΑΤΡΑΣ ....

d. ΚΟΡΙΝΘΟΣ ....

e. ΚΑΛΑΜΑΤΑ ....

f. ΒΟΛΟΣ ....

g. ΛΑΡΙΣΑ ....

h. ΡΟΔΟΣ ....

Did you know?

Traveling around in Greece

By air

Olympic Airways operates all its international and internal flights to the larger islands and main towns from the Western Terminal in Athens. Foreign airlines use the Eastern Terminal. A bus travels every 30 minutes between the two (travel time 10 minutes). The familiar names for the two airports are **i Olymbiakí** (the Olympic) and **i Anatolikí** (the Eastern). Certain routes are very busy and you are advised to book seats as early as possible. Reservation offices in Athens are at: 96, Singrou Avenue, 6, Othonos Street and at the Athens Hilton.

By rail

There are two main railway networks, each operated by the state company **OSE**. These networks are, however, limited. One serves parts of the north, linking with foreign networks. The other meanders southwards through the Peloponnese. There is also a line (**o elektrikós**) in Athens which runs between Piraeus – Athens – Kifissia. If you travel by train, reduced fares are available: a reduction of 20% on round-trip tickets, half-price fares for children and students and 2nd class touring cards for a set number of days and trips throughout the network may be advantageous to those traveling in small groups (2 – 15). In Athens there is a railway reservation office on Odos Sina (next door to the university).

By sea

There is an extensive network of ferries linking the mainland with the islands. Some of the nearer islands also have a hydrofoil service in the summer. Arrive early if you don't have a ticket and book in advance if possible.

By bus

Long-distance buses, which are colored turquoise, are efficient and reasonably priced. In Athens there are different bus stations (**praktoria**) according to which part of the country your destination is in – make sure you go to the right one! When you book the clerk will write your seat number on your ticket and your name on a chart for the conductor. Buses usually run on time but it can be difficult to find bus timetables in country areas. On the islands, buses will meet the ferries and timetables will change with ferry times.

By taxi

Rates are fixed by law and in town the driver must use his meter. Avoid sharing if possible but, if you do, note how much is on the meter when you get in. In the country you should agree on the price of the trip before setting out. There are long-distance taxis which are cheaper than the regular ones.

By car

If you are driving your own car, signs are quite good on main roads and destinations are printed in Greek with a transliteration into Latin script. There are only two superhighways on which you have to pay. Minor roads are often badly surfaced, with few signs, and garages are infrequent. Take a repair kit and only use 'super' gasoline. The Greek Automobile and Touring Club (**ELPA**) has patrols along main roads in yellow jeeps marked *Assistance Routière*. You can contact them near large towns by dialing 104 from any telephone. Foreigners are entitled to free legal and mechanical assistance, but parts are extra.

By rental car

You will need to produce your driver's license – an international license is not compulsory – and your passport. Make sure the rental contract includes sufficient insurance. You must be at least twenty-three years old to rent a car. Bikes, motorbikes and scooters are also available, but check the machine carefully – they are not always well maintained and can be unsafe.

Your turn to speak

In these two exercises you are going to practice making travel arrangements.

1   You are in Crete and you want to rent a car for five days. You will practice, **thelo na enikiaso** (I'd like to rent), **protimó** (I prefer), **poso ine tin imera?** (how much is it per day?) and **poso ine to hiliómetro?** (how much is it a kilometer?).

2   You want to book some tickets for an excursion but how far is it and what are the hotels like?

Revision/Review

Now turn to p. 217 and complete the revision section on Units 7–9. On the cassette *Revision* follows after this unit.

Answers

Practice what you have learned p. 127 Exercise 1 Patra, 1, 320 drahmés; Larisa, 3, 570 drahmés; Thessaloniki, 2, 900 drahmés.

p. 127 Exercise 2 a, c, e, g.

Grammar p. 129 (a) I want your passport   (b) Where is your hotel? (c) This is our car   (d) This is my suitcase   (e) We want our breakfast (f) Give me your passports   (g) Her chair is free   (h) My room is here.

The Greek alphabet p. 130 (a) Thessaloniki   (b) Athina   (c) Patras (d) Korinthos   (e) Kalamata   (f) Volos   (g) Larisa   (h) Rodos.

10 Food and drink

You will learn

- to cope with a Greek menu
- to order hors d'oeuvres
- to order main dishes
- to order things to drink

Before you begin

Follow the pattern of study set out below. The dialogues will introduce you to some Greek specialties which are explained in *Did you know?* As usual any new phrases are explained in the notes.

Study guide

	Dialogues 1–3: listen without the book
	Dialogues 1–3: listen, read and study one by one
	Dialogues 4–6 listen without the book
	Dialogues 4–6: listen, read and study one by one
	Study *Key words and phrases*
	Complete the exercises in *Practice what you have learned*
	Study *Grammar* and do the exercise
	Do *The Greek alphabet* and complete the exercise
	Read *Did you know?*
	Do the taped exercises in *Your turn to speak*
	Finally, listen to all the dialogues again.

Dialogues

1

Can the receptionist recommend a good taverna?

Mia tourístria	Borite na mou pite pou iparhi mia kalí taverna edó kondá?
Ipálilos	Ne, ine tris dromous pió kato, tha pate efthia ke ehi fresko psari ke kaló krasí.
Mia tourístria	Efharistó.
Ipalilos	Parakaló.

2

What is today's specialty?

Tourístria	Parakaló, pió ine to piato tis imeras?
Garsón	Ne, éhoume mousaká ke pastítsio.
Tourístria	Mia merida mousaká, parakaló.
Garsón	Endaksi, thélete típota alo?
Tourístria	Ke ena boukali krasí.
Garsón	Amesos.
Tourístria	Efharistó.
Garsón	Parakaló.

to piato dish, plate
to pastítsio macaroni pie
i merida portion

1 ♦ **borite na mou pite?** can you tell me? This is a very useful phrase.

pou iparhi mia kalí taverna edó kondá? where is there a good taverna near here?

♦ **tris dromous pió kato** three streets (roads) further down. 'Further up' is **pió epano.**

tha pate efthia go straight ahead (lit. you will go straight).

ehi fresko psari ke kaló krasí it has fresh fish and good wine.

2 ♦ **pió ine to piato tis imeras?** what's today's specialty? (lit. what's the dish of the day?). You can use this phrase or ask for the menu: **boró na do to katálogo?**

♦ **mia merida (mousaká)** a portion of (mousaka), but if you want two or more portions ask for **dio merides** (two portions), **tris merides** (three portions) etc. See *Did you know?* for Greek specialties.

Remember to use **mia** with feminine, **enas** with masculine and **ena** with neuter nouns.

3 *Yiannis and his mother are ordering lunch*

Yiannis Ti tha fame mamá?

Sofia Kítakse, yiá proto thelo na paro ena mousaká, mia salata na
pároume, ke metá na pároume kanena arnaki me patates sto
fourno, yiá sena mia koka kola, ke egó ena potiri krasí.

Yiannis '7 Up' thelo.

Sofia Kalá, pare '7 Up', ke egó ena potiri krasí, yiá mena. Ke metá,
yiá glikó borí na zitísoume ligo halvá, ti nomizis? Garsón. . .

i salata salad
metá after
to glikó candy, dessert
halva Greek candy (see *Did you know?*)

4 *Kiria Maria orders everything the waiter suggests*

Garsón Ke ta barboúnia?

Kiria Maria Ne.

Garsón Tin orea mas ti melidzanosalata?

Kiria Maria Ne.

Garsón Mia oréa melidzanosalata, to lahanaki to pikántiko, ena oréo
ohtapodi.

Kiria Maria Ne.

Garsón Ti domata. . . ti horiátiki.

Kiria Maria Ne, ne.

Garsón Kremidaki.

Kiria Maria Ne.

Garsón Piperiá, elitsa, tiraki apola.

Kiria Maria Ne.

Garsón Mou'pes. Tora ti tha piite?

Kiria Maria Krasaki.

Garsón Krasaki.

to barbouni red mullet
i melidzanosalata eggplant purée
to lahanaki cabbage
pikántiko spicy, hot
to ohtapodi octopus
i piperiá pepper
to tirí cheese

3 ♦ **ti tha fame (mamá)?** what shall we eat (Mummy)? The waiter will ask you **ti tha fate?** (what will you eat?). Your answer could be: **tha fao. . .** (I will eat. . .) or, if you are not alone, **tha fame. . .** (we will eat. . .).

kítakse look!

yiá proto for the first course (lit. for first).

ke metá na pároume and after let's have.

kanena arnaki me patates sto fourno some lamb with roast potatoes (lit. lamb with potatoes in the oven). 'Roast chicken' is **kotópoulo sto fourno**.

yiá sena for you. With **yiá** (for) use **sena** (you). 'For me' is **yiá mena** and 'for us' is **yiá mas**.

ena potiri krasí a glass of wine (lit. one glass wine). Remember that in phrases like these you do not need the 'of' in Greek e.g. **ena koutí spirta** (a box of matches).

borí na zitísoume we can ask for (lit. it is possible that we'll ask for).

ti nomizis? what do you think?

4 **ti domata. . . ti horiátiki (salata)** tomato. . . Greek (salad).
I horiátiki salata is literally a 'village salad' made with **domates** (tomatoes), **kremidi** (onions) **piperiá** (peppers), **eliés** (olives) and **feta** (Greek white cheese).

kremidaki onion (lit. little onion).

elitsa olive (lit. little olive). To make masculine and neuter nouns smaller you add **-aki**, but with feminine nouns you generally use **-itsa** or **-oula**.

mou'pes right, ok. **mou'pes** is short for **mou ipes** (lit. you've told me).

♦ **tora ti tha piite?** now what would you like to drink? (lit. what will you drink?). Your answer could be: **tha pio. . .** (I'll drink. . .) or, if you are not alone, **tha pioume. . .** (we'll drink. . .).

krasaki some wine (lit. a little wine).

5 Ordering hors d'oeuvres

Anna   Eh! Garsón.
Garsón   Ena leptó amesos érhoume.
Anna   Er, sas parakaló, ti éhete yiá orektiká?
Garsón   Ehi tirí feta, tirópites, er, salata, er, eliés. . .
Anna   Eh!... lipón, yiá ferte mas liyes elitses, tiraki, er ligo krasaki retsina. Esís ti thélete Tsela?
Tsela   Egó mia koka kola mono.
Garsón   Málista, amesos.

retsina resinated white wine

6 The salad is good, but what's the fish like?

Kiria Maria   Na sou valo ke liyi orea salata?
Eleni   Ne parakaló.
Kiria Maria   Polí orea salata. To psari ine na to tros ke na glipsis ta daktilá sou. Para polí oreo, nóstimo, nóstimo. . .

ta dáktila fingers
nóstimos-i-o tasty

5 **ena leptó amesos érhoume** just a moment I'm coming right away (lit. one minute right away I'm coming).

♦ **ti éhete yiá orektiká?** what do you have for hors d'oeuvres/appetizers?

ferte mas bring us. This is the normal phrase when ordering and is not as abrupt as it sounds in English.

liyes elitses a few olives.

6 ♦ **na sou valo?** may I serve you? (lit. may I put for you?). You can use the same expression for drinks e.g. **na sou valo krasí?** (may I pour you some wine?).

ke liyi orea salata a nice little salad, too.

ine na tros ke na glipsis ta daktilá sou it's absolutely delicious (lit. it's for eating and for licking your fingers).

Key words and phrases

To learn

boró na do to katálogo?	can I see the menu?
borite na mou pite?	can you tell me?
ti éhete yiá orektiká?	what do you have for hors d'oeuvres?
pió ine to piato tis imeras?	what is the dish of the day?
thelo na paro	I'd like to have
yiá proto	for the first course
mia merida mousaká	one portion of mousaka
dio merides pastítsio	two portions of macaroni pie
tris merides kotópoulo	three portions of chicken
horiátiki salata	Greek salad
melidzanosalata	eggplant purée
taramosalata	cod-roe purée
ohtapodi	octopus
barboúnia	red mullet
yiá glikó	for dessert
halvás	a Greek candy

To understand

ti tha fate?	what will you eat?
ti tha pite?	what will you drink?
na sou valo ligo/liyi. .?	may I serve you a little. .?
ti nomízete?	what do you think?

Practice what you have learned

Read the instructions to each exercise before switching on the tape. Each exercise is about ordering, eating or preparing food.

1 One item is out of place in each part of the menu below. Listen to the tape and tick the item which is the odd-man out. (Answers p. 146)

Orektiká

a. ☐ eliés

b. ☐ taramosalata

c. ☐ halvá

d. ☐ melidzanosalata

Prota

a. ☐ mousaká

b. ☐ pastítsio

c. ☐ tirí feta

d. ☐ domates yemistés

Psária

a. ☐ arnaki sto fourno

b. ☐ oktapodi

c. ☐ barboúnia

d. ☐ psari sto fourno

Salates

a. ☐ domata me kremidi

b. ☐ horiátiki

c. ☐ retsina

d. ☐ taramosalata

2 Nikos and Sofia are eating out. Listen to what each orders and match the food and drink with the correct person. (Answers p. 146)

3 The words in the sentences below are jumbled up. Listen to the
conversation and put the words in the right order.

Garsón fate tha ti? ....

Touristria mousaká thelo merida mia ....

....

Garsón den distihós eho ....

Touristria ine pió to piato imeras tis? ....

....

Garsón arnaki pastítsio sto fourno ke ....

....

Touristria sto fourno arnaki ....

Garsón ti piite tha? ....

Touristria potiri ena krasí ....

4 Look at the list below and tick off the ingredients you would need to make
a **horiátiki salata**. Check your selection with the tape.

☐ melidzanes

☐ eliés

☐ feta

☐ avgá

☐ ladi

☐ kremidi

☐ piperiá

☐ domates

☐ gala

☐ rizi

Grammar

Prepositions

You have now come across the most important prepositions:

apó	from	**metá**	after
se	to/in	**me**	with
yiá	for	**horís**	without

But it is important to remember that after these words the masculine and feminine words for 'the' change:

o becomes **to(n)**	masculine
i becomes **ti(n)**	feminine
to remains **to**	neuter

e.g. **apó ton Pirea**	from Piraeus
yiá tin Anglia	for England
metá to mesimeri	after midday
sto Londino	to London

The words for 'the' also change in the masculine and feminine plural:

i becomes **tous**	masculine
i becomes **tis**	feminine
ta remains **ta**	neuter

e.g. **me tous andres**	with the men
horis tis yinekes	without the women

Exercise

Translate the following sentences into English. (Answers p. 146)

a. I eliés ine apó tin Ellada ....

b. Símera pame stin Athina ....

c. To aeroplano fevgi yiá to Londino stis októ ....

d. Pao sti thálassa metá to yevma ....

e. O andras mou theli ouzo me neró ....

f. Egó thelo kafé horís záhari ....

g. Theloume mia horiátiki salata me to mousaká ....

h. I timí yiá to domátio ine horís proinó ....

Pino

The verb to note in this unit is **pino** (I drink)

pino	I drink	**pínoume**	we drink
pinis	you drink	**pínete**	you drink
pini	he/she/it drinks	**pínoune**	we drink

The Greek alphabet

Letters you have already met

A α	'a' as in father		M μ	'm' as in my
B β	'v' as in van		N ν	'n' as in never
Γ γ	'g' as in guild 'y' as in yet (before 'e' and 'i')		O o	'o' as in hot
			Π π	'p' as in pie
Δ δ	'd' as in door		P ρ	'r' as in red
E ε	'e' as in let		Σ σ ς	's' as in sand
Θ θ	'th' as in this		T τ	't' as in tip
I ι	'i' as in police		Φ φ	'f' as in four
K κ	'k' as in key		Ω ω	'o' as in hot
Λ λ	'l' as in live			

New letters

Letter	Name	Equivalent sound in English
H η	ita	'i' as in police
Ψ ψ	psi	'psi' as in tops

First cover the left-hand column and underline the new letters. Then uncover it and read the words out loud.

i	ή
Eleni	Ἑλένη
ílios	ἥλιος
imera	ἡμέρα
psari	ψάρι
psomí	ψωμί
Amerikí	Ἀμερική
Athina	Ἀθῆνα

Exercise Copy out this recipe for **mousaká** and translate the ingredients into English. (Answers p. 146)

1 κιλό μελιτζάνες	γάλα ....
1 κιλό κιμᾶ	ἁλάτι ....
2 ντομάτες	πιπέρι ....
1 κρεμμύδι	τυρί ....
2 αὐγά	ἀλέυρι ....
βούτιρο	

Did you know?

Eating out

The traditional place to eat out in the evening is the **taverna**. Here you can order a range of dishes for **mezé** (appetizer) such as **taramosalata** (smoked cod-roe purée), **melidzanosalata** (eggplant mashed with lemon and garlic), **gigandes** (bean salad in a tomato sauce), **keftedes** (meatballs), **loukánika** (Greek sausages) and **horiátiki salata** (tomato salad with onions, olives and **feta**). The usual main dishes are grilled steak, chops and **souvlákia** (kebabs). There may also be **bifteki** which is a grilled hamburger; steak is called **bonfilé**. Many tavernas do not have a menu so it is best to follow the Greek practice of going into the kitchen to choose what you want to eat. Most tavernas sell draft **retsina** which is served in little yellow cans or carafes and sold by weight (a kilo = a liter). **Retsina** gets its distinctive taste from the addition of resin to the barrels during fermentation. Many people who acquire a taste for **retsina** can't envisage life without it, but you can always buy unresinated white and red wines like Demestica and Hymettos and bottled lagers. If there is a wine waiter (he will also serve the water and the bread), a small tip should be left on the table (not the plate with the bill). Tavernas with music are more expensive.

In a **psárotaverna** (fish taverna) you will find various fish according to the season and shellfish like **garides** (prawns), **karavides** (crayfish) and sometimes **astakós** (lobster). After you have chosen your fish it is weighed to give the price before it is cooked (lobster and large fish are expensive). The **psistariá** is like the taverna but specializes in grilled meat. There are also many restaurants (**estiatório**) which vary greatly – some serve international cuisine and others are virtually indistinguishable from tavernas. If the menu lists two prices for each item the second price includes 10% service, but an extra tip is always welcome. Most tavernas and restaurants do not serve sweets or coffee so it is customary to go on to a **kafenio** (café) or **zaharoplastio** (pastry shop) to round off the meal. Finally, there are a number of little places you can go to drink and eat titbits: a **koutouki** for wine and an **ouzeri** for ouzo. These are friendly and informal – some have only three or four tables – and excellent places to practice your Greek.

Your turn to speak

In this section we'll be asking you to take part in two conversations where you can practice ordering different sorts of food. Remember to read the instructions to each exercise and then work with the tape alone. Alexandros will tell you what to say.

1 You are in a small taverna with your husband/wife and two children. Order the meals for all of you. You'll be able to practice **pió ine to piato tis imeras?** (what is today's special?), **mia merida mousaká** (a portion of mousaka) and **ena boukali krasí** (a bottle of wine).

2 You are in a restaurant in Plaka with your husband/wife. This time you'll be able to practice **boró na do to katálogo?** (can I look at the menu?), **ti éhete yiá orektiká?** (what are the hors d'oeuvres?) and **to logariasmó** (the bill).

Answers

Practice what you have learned p. 141 Exercise 1 halva, tiri feta, arnaki sto fourno, retsina.

p. 141 Exercise 2 Niko: taramosalata, mousaká, patates, kókkino krasí. Sofia: melidzanosalata, barboúnia, horiátiki salata, retsina.

Grammar p. 143 (**a**) The olives are from Greece (**b**) Today we are going to Athens (**c**) The plane leaves for London at eight (**d**) I'm going to the sea after lunch (**e**) My husband would like ouzo with water (**f**) I'd like coffee without sugar (**g**) We'd like a Greek salad with the mousaka (**h**) The price for the room is without breakfast.

The Greek alphabet p. 144 1 kilo of eggplant, 1 kilo of mincemeat, 2 tomatoes, 1 onion, 2 eggs, butter, milk, salt, pepper.

11 Likes and dislikes

You will learn

- to say you like or don't like something
- to say how much you like something
- to state preferences
- to talk about the weather

Before you begin

Follow the pattern of study set out below. Pay particular attention to the verb **aresi** which is used to say you like something.

Study guide

	Dialogues 1, 2: listen without the book
	Dialogues 1, 2: listen, read and study one by one
	Dialogues 3–5: listen without the book
	Dialogues 3–5: listen, read and study one by one
	Study *Key words and phrases*
	Complete the exercises in *Practice what you have learned*
	Study *Grammar* and do the exercise
	Do *The Greek alphabet* and complete the exercise
	Read *Did you know?*
	Do the taped exercises in *Your turn to speak*
	Finally, listen to all the dialogues again

Dialogues

1 *Do you prefer Greek coffee or nescafé?*

Anna   Laki, sou aresi o ellinikós kafés?
Lakis   Ohi, protimó to nescafé me gala . . . Anna, sou aresi to podósfero?
Anna   Ohi Laki, protimó to tennis.
Lakis   Anna ti protimás, kreas i psari?
Anna   Protimó kreas Laki, de mou aresoun ta psária.

to podósfero football
to kreas meat

2 *What else do you like?*

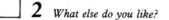

Maria   Sou aresi polí to karpouzi?
Katerina   Ah! Ne, m'aresi para polí to karpouzi. S'aresi o mousakás?
Maria   Ne, polí.
Katerina   Ke ti ala fayitá sou aresoun polí?
Maria   Er, mou aresi to kotópoulo me patates tiganités.
Katerina   Er, emena mou aresi na tro kreas me kolokíthia, alá to tro ke me tis melidzanes.
Maria   Emena mou aresi i taramosalata.
Katerina   Ah! Egó protimó ti horiátiki salata me tirí feta mesa . . . sto trapezi esís pínete krasí to mesimeri?
Maria   Ne, pínoume. Egó protimó to áspro krasí.
Katerina   Ah! Ego protimó na pio ouzo ligo prin apó to fayitó mou.

to karpouzi watermelon
to kotópoulo chicken
i patates tiganités fried potatoes, French fries
ta kolokíthia zucchini

1 ◆ **sou aresi?** do you like? (lit. does it please you?). **Aresi** (it pleases) is used in two forms only: **aresi** (it pleases) and **aresoun** (they please) e.g. **sou aresi o kafés?** (do you like coffee?), **sou aresi i Ellada?** (do you like Greece?), **sou aresoun i sokolates?** (do you like chocolates?), **sou aresoun i salates?** (do you like salads?). **Sou** (to you) is used when speaking to children or friends and is sometimes shortened to **s'** e.g. **s'aresi o kafés.** You should usually use **sas** (to you) to be polite e.g. **sas aresi i Ellada?** (do you like Greece?).

kreas i psari meat or fish. Here **i** means 'or'.

◆ **de mou aresoun ta psária** I don't like fish (lit. they do not please me the fish). **Mou** can be shortened to **m'** e.g. **m'aresi to kreas** (I like meat). Note that the word for 'not' **de(n)** comes before the **mou.**

2 ◆ **m'aresi para polí** I like very much indeed. Remember how **para** is used to strengthen **polí** e.g. **efharistó para polí** thank you very much indeed.

◆ **ti ala fayitá sou aresoun polí?** what other foods do you like very much? Note that because **fayitó** (food, meal) is in the plural form **fayitá** (foods, meals) you use **aresoun** (they please).

emena me. Like **egó, emena** is used for emphasis before a verb

◆ **mou aresi na tro** I like to eat. You could turn this into a question: **sas aresi na trote kreas?** do you like to eat meat? **Tro** (I eat) is found in *Grammar*, Unit 12.

alá to tro ke me tis melidzanes but I eat it (meat) with eggplant too.

sto trapezi esís pínete krasí to mesimeri? do you drink wine at lunch? (lit. at table do you drink wine at midday?).

egó protimó na pió ouzo ligo prin apó to fayitó mou I prefer to drink ouzo a little before my meal.

3 *Anna and Lakis escape the rain by going to a taverna*

Lakis Psihalizi.
Anna Pame se mia taverna?
Lakis Ne, pame.
Anna Aftí i taverna ehi freska psária ke kaló krasí.
Lakis Kani krio símera.
Anna Ne, kani polí krio, de mou aresi o fetinós himonas, ine polí varís.

4 *Tsela only likes certain Greek foods*

Anna De mou les, s'aresoun ta elliniká fayitá?
Tsela Orismena, ne.
Anna Diladí, ti sou aresi pió polí?
Tsela Er, mou aresi to pastítsio, ke to souvlaki.
Anna Ah! . . . polí oréa.

5 *It's too hot in Athens, so Anna suggests a trip to Nafplio*

Lakis Kani polí zesti símera. Pame sti thálassa?
Anna De mou aresi i Athina to kalokeri, kani panda polí zesti. Pame sto Nafplio, eki ine polí oréo.

to kalokeri summer

3 ♦ **psihalizi** it's drizzling. Also, **vrehi** (it's raining) and **hionizi** (it's snowing).

pame se mia taverna let's go to a taverna.

♦ **kani krio símera** it's cold today (lit. it makes cold). 'It's hot' is **kani zesti**. 'The weather' is **o keros**.

♦ **o fetinós himonas** winter this year (lit. this year's winter). Like other adjectives **fetinós** changes according to the gender of the noun it is describing: **i ániksi** (the spring) is feminine, so 'this year's spring' is **i fetiní ániksi, to kalokeri** (the summer, lit. the fine weather) is neuter and 'this year's summer' is **to fetinó kalokeri**. Autumn is **to fthinóporo**.

ine polí varís it is very hard.

4 **de mou les** tell me (lit. won't you tell me). This is a very common way of starting a question; the polite form is **de mou lete**.

orismena some/certain. Here this adjective ends in **-a** because it refers to the neuter plural **ta fayitá** (foods).

diladí that's to say/in other words. Some other examples of this useful word: **doulevo sto tahidromio, diladí ime ipálilos** (I work at the post office, in other words I'm an employee), **diladí prepi na pao símera** (in other words, I must go today).

ti sou aresi pió polí? what do you like best?

to souvlaki shish kebab (skewered grilled meat). The word for 'skewer' is **souvla**, so **to souvlaki** is literally 'a little skewer'.

5 ♦ **kani polí zesti (símera)** it is very hot (today). Remember the use of **kani** to say what the weather's like.

♦ **kani panda polí zesti** it's always very hot.

♦ **ekí ine polí oreo** it's very nice there. You can see in these last units how frequently the Greeks use the word **oreo/orea**.

Key words and phrases

To learn

mou aresi i Ellada	I like Greece
mou aresoun ta psária	I like fish
mou aresi na tro	I like to eat
mou aresi na pio	I like to drink
mou aresi i ániksi	I like the spring
to kalokeri	summer
to fthinóporo	autumn
o himonas	winter
kani krio	it's cold
kani zesti	it's hot
vrehi	it's raining
psihalizi	it's drizzling
hionizi	it's snowing
mou aresi polí	I like very much
mou aresi para polí	I like very much indeed
de mou aresi	I don't like
de mou aresi katholou	I don't like at all

To understand

sas aresi i Ellada?	do you like Greece?
sas aresi to kalokeri?	do you like the summer?
sas aresoun ta elliniká fayitá?	do you like Greek food?
ti fayitá sas aresoun?	what food do you like?
diladí, ti sou aresi pió polí?	in other words, what do you like best?
orismena	some, certain
to podósfero	soccer

Practice what you have learned

Read the instructions for each exercise before switching on the tape. You are going to hear about people's likes and dislikes and the weather.

1 Anna and Lakis are talking about their preferences using the verb **protimó** (I prefer). Listen to the tape and, using the spaces provided, fill in *how much* they like and dislike certain things using **polí** (a lot), **para polí** (very much indeed), **ligo** (a little) and **katholou** (not at all).

	psária	kreas	ouzo	podósfero
Anna				
Yiannis				

2 Here you have a conversation in a taverna. Listen to the tape and then complete the conversation with the words below.

Petros   Eleni, sou .... ta .... fayitá?

Eleni   .... ne

Petros   .... ti sou aresi .... polí?

Eleni   M'aresoun ta ...., ...

pastítsio, o ....

Petros   ...., de mou aresoun .... ta

psária

Eleni   Emena mou aresi .... polí to ohtapodi

Petros   Ohi, egó .... to .... me ....

Eleni   Egó protimó ta barboúnia me horiátiki ....

protimó   salata   para   mousakás   díladí

orismena   katholou   kreas   barboúnia   to

aresoun   pió   emena   patates   elliniká

3 What's the weather like in different European countries? Listen to the tape and fill in the weather report. Then translate the name of the country and the report into English. (Answers p. 158)

	Country	Weather report
Anglia		
Ispania		
Yermania		
Gallia		
Italia		
Ellada		
Ollandia		
Dania		

Grammar

Just verbs

You have already come across a number of verbs in the present tense. These fall into two main groups:

1 In the first group the stress is on the next-to-the-last syllable in the singular e.g.

katalaveno	I understand	**katalavénoume**	we understand
katalavenis	you understand	**katalavénete**	you understand
katalaveni	he/she/it understands	**katalavénoune**	they understand

Other verbs in this group include:

dino	I give	**kano**	I do	**piano**	I take
doulevo	I work	**kriono**	I'm cold	**pino**	I drink
eho	I have	**meno**	I stay/live	**thelo**	I want
fevgo	I leave	**nomizo**	I think		

2 In the second group the stress is on the last syllable in the singular e.g.

miló	I speak	**milame**	we speak
milás	you speak	**milate**	you speak
milái	he/she/it speaks	**milane**	they speak

Other verbs in this group include:

kitó	I look	**perpató**	I walk
kolimbó	I swim	**protimó**	I prefer
pernó	I pass	**rotó**	I ask

Of course, there are a number of irregular verbs, some of which you already know and some which you will learn in the next unit.

Exercise Complete the sentences using **thelo**, **miló**, **pao** or **boró** changing the endings to fit the person. (Answers p. 158)

a. I María .... dio grammatósima.

b. To pedí .... kalá elliniká.

c. I Anna ke i Sofia .... barbounia ke egó

.... kreas.

d. O andras mou ke egó .... stin Ellada.

e. Ne, i yineka mou .... polí kalá ta elliniká.

f. .... na pame stin Anglia, alá de théloume na

pame.

The Greek alphabet

Letters you have already met

A α	'a' as in father		M μ	'm' as in my
B β	'v' as in van		N ν	'n' as in never
Γ γ	'g' as in guild 'y' as in yet (before 'e' and 'i')		O o	'o' as in hot
			Π π	'p' as in pie
Δ δ	'd' as in door		P ρ	'r' as in red
E ε	'e' as in let		Σ σ ς	's' as in send
H η	'i' as in police		T τ	't' as in tip
Θ θ	'th' as in this		Φ φ	'f' as in four
I ι	'i' as in police		Ψ ψ	'ps' as in tops
K κ	'k' as in key		Ω ω	'o' as in hot
Λ λ	'l' as in live			

New letters

Letter	Name	Equivalent sound in English
Z ζ	zita	'z' as in zoo
Y υ	ipsilon	'i' as in police

First cover the left-hand column and underline the new letters. Then uncover it and read the words out loud.

záhari	ζάχαρη
signomi	συγγνώμη
zoí	ζωή
zesti	ζέστη
varís	βαρύς
sinántisi	συνάντηση
yemizo	γεμίζω
yiro	γύρω
distihós	δυστυχώς
diavazo	διαβάζω

Exercise Here is a list of capital cities. Write down the countries whose capitals they are in the spaces below. (Answers p. 158)

a. Άμστερνταμ ....
b. Βιέννη ....
c. Βρουξέλλες ....
d. Λονδίνο ....
e. Μαδρίτη ....

f. Μόσχα ....
g. Όσλο ....
h. Παρίσι ....
i. Ρώμη ....
j. Τόκιο ....

Did you know?

Athens and Attica

Of Greece's total population (about 9.5 million), over a third live in the
Athens-Piraeus area. The massive migration from the countryside and the
rapid and unplanned expansion of the two cities have led to an ugly urban
sprawl. Regrettably, although ancient sites have been protected, many fine
old buildings of the last century have been demolished. However, it is still
possible to find some pleasant oases in the daunting sea of concrete and
there are, of course, ancient and Byzantine sites which are of exceptional
beauty and interest. The **Acropolis**, the **Agora**, the **Theatre of Dionysus**
and the National Archeological, Byzantine and Benaki Museums obviously
should not be missed. Always check opening times of museums and sites
before you visit – some are closed on Mondays or Tuesdays. It is also well
worth wandering around the old quarter of Plaka during the day – before
the nightlife starts up – and climbing to the **Philoppapou Monument** on
the hill opposite the Parthenon from which you can get a magnificent view
of the Acropolis. If you want to escape from the city for a few hours there
are the Byzantine monasteries at **Kaisariani**, on the slopes of Mount
Hymettos and the church at **Daphni** with its exquisite twelfth century
mosaics. You can also take longer excursions to **Delphi** (the seat of the
Delphic Oracle), **Marathon** (where you can still see the burial mound of the
192 Athenians killed when Athens defeated the Persians in 490 BC) and
Cape Sounion (the site of the Temple of Poseidon).

There are both beaches that are free and those where you pay all along
the coast from Piraeus to Sounion – however, the sea near the city is very
polluted so it's best to go at least as far as Vouliagmeni to swim.
Alternatively you can take the short ferry trip to the island of **Aegina** (a
much less tiring trip than the drive along the busy coast road).

There is a wide choice of places to eat in Athens, although some tavernas
close for the summer. Between Piraeus and Faliron there is the delightful
little port of **Tourkolimano** (Mikrolimano) which is lined with restaurants
serving excellent fresh fish.

Your turn to speak

In the conversations on the tape you are going to state your preferences and ask someone else theirs. Remember to read the information for each exercise and then work with the tape alone.

1 You are sitting in a bar with a glass of ouzo when a man speaks to you. You are going to practice: **mou aresi** (I like), **de mou aresi** (I don't like) and **protimó** (I prefer).

2 You want to practice some of the words you know for Greek food. You are going to practice: **protimó** (I prefer), **diladí** (in other words), **ti sas aresi** like best?) and **polí orea souvlákia** (very good kebabs).

Tourkolimano (Mikrolimano)

Answers

12 More about yourself

You will learn

- to understand and reply to questions about yourself and your family
- to understand and reply to questions about your knowledge of Greek
- when to use polite and familiar terms
- some irregular verbs

Before you begin

Follow the pattern of study set out in the *Study guide* below. Pay particular attention to the ways of answering and asking questions politely of people you don't know well. You will notice that some of the most useful words and phrases from the earlier units are used again in the dialogues.

Study guide

	Dialogues 1–3: listen without the book
	Dialogues 1–3: listen, read and study one by one
	Dialogues 4–7: listen without the book
	Dialogues 4–7: listen, read and study one by one
	Study *Key words and phrases*
	Complete the exercises in *Practice what you have learned*
	Study *Grammar* and do the exercise
	Do *The Greek alphabet* and complete the exercise
	Read *Did you know?*
	Do the taped exercises in *Your turn to speak*
	Listen to all the dialogues again
	Finally, do *Revision/Review Units 9–12* at the end of the book

Dialogues

1 *Do you speak Greek?*

Marina	Milás ellitiká?
Eleni	Katalaveno alá de milao kalá.
Marina	O andras sou milai galliká?
Eleni	Milai arketá galliká ke liga ellitiká.

arketá a fair amount
galliká French

2 *Anna likes Athens more every time she visits it*

Lakis	Sou aresi i Athina?
Anna	Ne, ine polí orea.
Lakis	Proti forá érhese?
Anna	Ohi, eho erthí ales tris forés alá kathe forá mou aresi perisótero.

Plaka

1 ♦ **milás elliniká?** do you speak Greek? Use **milás** with friends and children. Here is another example: **thelis kafé?** (would you like coffee?). To be more polite and formal you would say **milate elliniká?** and **thélete kafé?**

♦ **de milao kalá** I don't speak well. **Milao** is an alternative form of **miló.**

♦ **o andras sou milai galliká?** does your husband speak French? **Milai** is an alternative form of **milá.**

milai arketá galliká ke liga elliniká he speaks a fair amount of French and a little Greek. Here are other uses of **arketá** and **liga: den eho arketá leftá** (I haven't enough money), **eho liga leftá** (I have a little money).

2 ♦ **proti forá érhese?** is this the first time you've come? (lit. First time do you come?) **Érhese** is a part of the verb **érhoume** (I come) which you will find in *Grammar* in this unit.

eho erthí ales tris forés I have been three times before (lit. I have come another three times). This is the past tense, but don't worry about it now.

♦ **kathe forá mou aresi perisótero** every time it pleases me more. Instead of **perisótero** you could say **pió polí** (see Unit 8, *Grammar*).

3 *Yiannis wants to get to know Maria better*

Yiannis	De mou les, pos se lene?
Maria	Me lene Maria,
Yiannis	Pou menis?
Maria	Sto Paleó Fáliro
Yiannis	Ise pandremeni?
Maria	Ohi, ime eléftheri.

4 *Maria welcomes Vivi to her house and asks her some questions about herself and her family*

Maria	Kalós orísate.
Vivi	Kalós sas vríkame.
Maria	Apó pou ísaste?
Vivi	Apó tin Afstralia.
Maria	Sas aresi i Ellada?
Vivi	Ne para polí.
Maria	Éhete keró stin Ellada?
Vivi	Mono dio meres.
Maria	O andras sas apó pou ine?
Vivi	Ine Amerikanós.
Maria	Éhete pediá?
Vivi	Ne, tria.
Maria	Ti ine korítsia i agória?
Vivi	Ine dio korítsia ke ena agori.
Maria	O andras sas ti douliá kani?
Vivi	Ine kathiyitís sto panepistímio.

3   **de mou les** tell me (see Unit 11, dialogue 4).

♦ **pou menis?** where do you live? The polite form is **pou ménete?** Your reply could be **meno stin Anglia** (I live in England). Remember to use the article in front of names.

♦ **ise pandremeni** are you married? The words for 'single' (lit. free) are: **eléftheros** for a man and **eléftheri** for a woman. Remember the ending **-i** is for feminine adjectives and **-os** for the masculine e.g. **i kali yineka** (the good woman), **o megalos andras** (the big man).

4 ♦ **kalós orísate** welcome!

♦ **kalós sas vríkame** glad to be here (lit. good to find you). You should use this phrase whenever somebody says **kalos orísate**.

♦ **éhete keró stin Ellada?** have you been in Greece long? (lit. have you time. . .).

mono dio meres only two days.

ti ine korítsia i agória? what are they, girls or boys?

ine kathiyitís sto panepistímio he is a professor/lecturer at the university. **Kathiyitís** (and its feminine form **kathiyítria**) also means 'school master, secondary school teacher'.

5 *Anna is at the hotel reception*

Anna	Yiá sou.
Yiorgos	Yiá sou. De mou les, pos se lene?
Anna	Me lene Anna. Esena pos se lene?
Yiorgos	Me lene Yiorgo.
Anna	Ise mono sou stin Ellada?
Yiorgos	Ohi, me ti yineka mou.
Anna	Ah. . . . ise pandremenos?
Yiorgos	Ne.

6 *Viky was born in Athens but now she's working in London*

Yiorgos	Viky, ise apó tin Athina?
Viky	Ne yeníthika stin Athina alá tora meno stin Anglia.
Yiorgos	Se pió meros?
Viky	Sto Londino.
Yiorgos	Ke ti douliá kanis?
Viky	Ime grammatévs.

7 *Viky is admiring Maria's baby*

Viky	Kalimera ti oreo moró!
Maria	Kalimera, apó pou ísaste?
Viky	Ime Anglida.
Maria	Milate elliniká polí orea.
Viky	Ne? Efharistó. O andras mou ine Éllinas. Pos to lene to moró sas?
Maria	Kosta.
Viky	Poso hronón ine?
Maria	Enámisi.
Viky	Mia hará ine, na sas zisi.
Maria	Efharistó polí. Hárika, hárika polí, andio sas.
Viky	K'egó episis, andio.

5 ♦ **yiá sou** hello. This is one of the most common greetings. Do you remember the polite form **yiá sas?**

esena (or **esí**) you. Used only for emphasis e.g. **esena ti sou aresi?** (what do *you* like?), **esí ti kanis?** (what are *you* doing?). **Esás** or **esís** are used with people you don't know well e.g. **esás pos sas lene?** (what's *your* name?).

♦ **ise monos sou?** are you on your own/alone? **Monos** means 'alone' in the masculine; if you are talking to a woman you would say **moni** e.g. **ise moni sou edó?** (are you alone here?), **ne, ime moni mou** (yes, I'm alone).

6 ♦ **alá tora meno stin Anglia** but now I live in England. Remember that **meno** means both 'I live' and 'I stay'.

♦ **se pió meros?** in which place?

ime grammatévs I'm (a) secretary.

7 ♦ **ti oreo moró** what a beautiful baby.

enámisi one and a half (see Unit 6, dialogue 3).

♦ **mia hará** lovely, wonderful. You can use this phrase if you are asked how you are, how your work is going etc. For example: **ti kánete?** (how are you?), **mia hará!** (fine!).

♦ **na sas zisi** may he/she live for you. This is said to parents at births, christenings, namedays and when you are admiring their children. (It is also said when people show photographs of members of their families.) If there is more than one child you say **na sas zisoun** (may they live for you).

Key words and phrases

To learn

milao liga elliniká	I speak a little Greek
eho erthí ales forés	I have been (here) before
kathe forá mou aresi pió polí	every time it pleases me more
ime me ton andra mou	I'm with my husband
ti yineka mou	my wife
kalós sas vríkame	glad to be here
yiá sou/sas	hello, good-bye
hárika polí	it was nice meeting you

To understand

kalós orísate	welcome
de mou lete	tell me
milate elliniká?	do you speak Greek?
protí forá érhese?	is this the first time you've come?
iste pandremenos?	are you married? (man)
iste pandremeni?	are you married? (woman)
iste eléftheros/eléftheri?	are you single?
iste monos/moni sou?	are you alone?
éhete keró stin Ellada?	have you been in Greece long?
pou ménete?	where do you live/are you staying?
se pió meros?	in which place?
na sas zisi	may he/she live for you
na sas zisoun	may they live for you
mia hará!	lovely, fine!

Practice what you have learned

Remember not to switch on the tape until you have read the instructions.

1 Listen to the tape and fill in the blanks below each picture.

Me lene .... **ime** .... **yeníthika stin** ....

Me lene .... **ime** .... **eho** .... **pediá**

Me lene .... **ime** .... **stin** ....

2 Complete this conversation using the sentences below. Then listen to the tape for the correct version.

Petros Yiá sou

Anna ....

Petros Apó pou ise?

Anna ....

Petros Ehis keró stin Ellada?

Anna ....

Petros Milás polí kalá ta elliniká.

Anna ....

Petros Ise moni sou edó?

Anna ....

Petros Ah! ise pandremeni. . .

> efharistó   ohi, me ton andra mou   apó tin Anglia
>
> yiá sou   tris meres

3 Petros is using the polite forms of words to Maria as he doesn't know her well. Underline what he should say. (We have done the first line for you.) Check with the tape for the rest of the conversation.

Petros Ehis keró stin Ellada? <u>Éhete keró stin Ellada?</u>

Maria Deka meres.

Petros Sas aresi?/Sou aresi?

Maria Ne, polí.

Petros Apó pou ise?/Apó pou ísaste?

Maria Apó tin Anglia.

Petros Ísaste moni sas?/Ise moni sou?

Maria Ohi, me ton andra mou.

Petros Éhete pediá?/Ehis pediá?

Maria Ohi.

Petros O andras sas ti douliá kani?/O andras sou ti douliá kani?

Maria Ine kathiyitís.

4 Listen to the tape and complete the two conversations below. The first is between two people talking formally, the second between two teenagers.

Kirios Kalimera ...., kiria ....

Kiria Eleni .... sas, ti ....?

Kirios .... kalá, ke ....?

Kiria Eleni Etsi ki .... Ime ligo ....

Lakis .... mou les, ... se

.... ?

Anna Me .... Anna.

Lakis Ti ....?

Anna Kalá, ...

Lakis .... kalá.

Grammar

Polite and familiar forms

You have learned that there are two ways of saying 'you' in Greek, a 'polite' form for people you don't know well or for when you are talking to more than one person and a 'familiar' form for speaking to friends, relatives and children:

polite	*familiar*	
thélete típota?	**thelis típota?**	do you want anything?
ti kánete?	**ti kanis?**	how do you do?

There are also two forms if you want to use 'you' as the object of a verb:

sas katalaveno	**se katalaveno**	I understand you
sas theloun	**se theloun**	they want you

To say 'to you' **sas** remains the same but **se** changes to **sou:**

sas miló	**sou miló**	I'm speaking to you
sas dinoun	**sou dinoun**	they give (to) you

In general you should use the polite form of the verb (**-ete/-ate**) and personal pronoun (**sas**). However, if the atmosphere is informal or you get to know someone well and they use the familiar form of the verb (**-is/-as**) and the personal pronouns (**se/sou**) when speaking to you, you should follow suit. Country people outside the towns tend to be more informal and simply use the familiar 'you' when speaking to one person and the plural 'you' when addressing more than one person. If in doubt stick to the polite form with adults, but always use the familiar form with children.

More verbs

Here are three more useful verbs. They are all irregular.

érhoume	I come	**erhómaste**	we come
érhese	you come	**érheste**	you come
érhete	he/she/it comes	**érhounte**	they come

leo	I say	**leme**	we say
les	you say	**lete**	you say
lei	he/she/it says	**lene**	they say

tro	I eat	**trome**	we eat
tros	you eat	**trote**	you eat
troi	he/she/it eats	**trone**	they eat

Exercise Complete these sentences using **thelo** (I want), **érhoume** (I come), **katalaveno** (I understand), **aresi** (it pleases) and **tro** (I eat). Then translate the sentences into English. (Answers p. 172)

a. .... stis deka i ora ....

b. .... psária kathe mera ....

c. .... alá de milao kalá ....

d. .... ena tsigaro ....

e. Mou .... polí i retsina ....

The Greek alphabet

Letters you have already met

A α	'a' as in father		M μ	'm' as in my
B β	'v' as in van		N ν	'n' as in never
Γ γ	'g' as in guild 'y' as in yet (before 'e' and 'i')		O o	'o' as in hot
			Π π	'p' as in pie
Δ δ	'd' as in door		P ρ	'r' as in red
E ε	'e' as in let		Σ σ ς	's' as in send
Z ζ	'z' as in zoo		T τ	't' as in tip
H η	'i' as in police		Y υ	'i' as in police
Θ θ	'th' as in this		Φ φ	'f' as in four
I ι	'i' as in police		Ψ ψ	'ps' as in tops
K κ	'k' as in key		Ω ω	'o' as in hot
Λ λ	'l' as in live			

New letters

Letter	Name	Equivalent sound in English
Ξ ξ	ksi	'ks' as in tricks
X χ	hi	'ch' as in Bach or, if you can't make this sound, a fairly forceful 'h' as in help

First cover the left-hand column and underline the new letters. Then uncover it and read the words out loud.

hérete	χαίρετε
hiliómetro	χιλιόμετρο
deksiá	δεξιά
hroma	χρωμα
hthes	χθές
hionizi	χιονίζει
eksi	ἔξι

Exercise Here is a list of countries. Write down the English equivalents in the spaces provided. (Answers p. 172)

a. Ἰνδία ....   e. Ἰρλανδία ....

b. Λουξεμβοῦργο ....   f. Γαλλία ....

c. Σκωτία ....   g. Πορτογαλία ....

d. Αὐστραλία ....   h. Καναδᾶς ....

Did you know?

Northern Greece

Greece's second largest city, Thessaloniki, lies in the heart of the northern region. The atmosphere here is more relaxed and the pace of life less hectic than in Athens. Although the town is an industrial center it has some attractive features – such as its waterfront cafés and restaurants – and is a pleasant place to stay. Also, Thessaloniki's central position makes it an ideal base for visiting the rest of the region. The area is rich in archeological remains and the ancient theatres at **Philippi** and on the island of **Thassos** are used for productions during the summer. The most exciting recent discovery is the unplundered royal tomb at **Vergina** which is probably that of Philip of Macedon, the father of Alexander the Great.

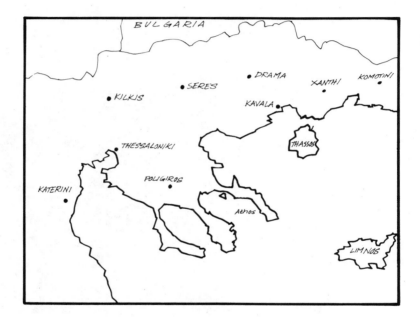

The North is notable for its lively folk traditions. Of particular interest are the ceremonies of the Anestanarides or firewalkers who celebrate the anniversary of their patron saints St. Constantine and St. Eleni (May 21) by walking barefoot on red-hot coals carrying their ikon on three successive evenings.

The region includes a theocratic 'state', **Mt. Athos** (the Eastern prong of the three peninsulas of Halkidiki). Women and even female animals are banned, but the many monasteries and hermitages offer hospitality to male visitors. In order to enter the 'Holy Mountain' it is necessary to obtain a permit from the authorities in Thessaloniki.

East of Mt. Athos there is the pleasant town of **Kavala** which has a well-preserved Roman aqueduct and Byzantine fortress. From Kavala there is a ferry to nearby Thassos which is a lovely, thickly wooded island with fine sandy beaches.

Your turn to speak

When you're in Greece you should listen carefully to the way others address you and then use the same form with them. These two conversations will give you a chance to use polite and familiar forms. In the first you're going to practice **yiá sou** (hello), **pos se lene?** (what's your name?) and **apó pou ise?** (where are you from?). In the second you will be more formal and use **thélete ena potiri krasí?** (would you like a glass of wine?) and **ísaste pandremeni?** (are you married?).

1 You've just arrived at your hotel and go to the disco. It's full of young people who will speak to you informally using **ise?** (are you?) and **kanis** (you do). You don't want to appear unfriendly so you should use the form they use.

2 Here you are at a very formal party. You don't know the woman next to you. She politely asks you some questions about yourself. You should reply politely using **thélete?** (would you like?) and **ísaste?** (are you?).

Monastery of Simopetra, Mt. Athos

Revision/Review

Now turn to p. 218 and complete the revision section on Units 10–12. On the cassette *Revision* follows after this unit.

Answers

Grammar p. 169 (**a**) I'm coming at ten o'clock (**b**) I eat fish every day (**c**) I understand but I don't speak well (**d**) I'd like a cigarette (**e**) I like retsina very much.

The Greek alphabet p. 169 (**a**) India (**b**) Luxembourg (**c**) Scotland (**d**) Australia (**e**) Ireland (**f**) France (**g**) Portugal (**h**) Canada.

13 The Greek alphabet

You will learn

- to use your knowledge of the Greek alphabet
- to ask where to make a telephone call
- to make a telephone call
- to understand sentences in the past tense

Before you begin

In the first four dialogues you will learn how to ask where to make a telephone call and how to ask for the directory. The other dialogues concentrate mainly on the sounds in the Greek alphabet, especially useful if you have to spell your name or your hotel. As usual you should follow the study pattern set out below.

Study guide

	Dialogues 1–4: listen without the book
	Dialogues 1–4: listen, read and study one by one
	Dialogues 5–7: listen without the book
	Dialogues 5–7: listen, read and study one by one
	Study *Key words and phrases*
	Complete the exercises in *Practice what you have learned*
	Study *Grammar*
	Do *The Greek alphabet*
	Read *Did you know?*
	Do the taped exercises in *Your turn to speak*
	Finally, listen to all the dialogues again

Dialogues

1 *Katerina wants to know if there is a public telephone nearby*

Katerina Thelo na tilefoniso, er, iparhi edó kondá períptero i tilefonikós thálamos?
Maria Ne, iparhi períptero, ine ligo pió kato apo'dó, olo efthia tha pate.
Katerina Efharistó.
Maria Parakaló.

2 *Anna wants to find a phone number but needs the directory and the yellow pages*

Anna Parakaló, éhete tilefonikó katálogo?
Kírios Ne, oriste.
Anna Efharistó. Tha íthela ke to hrisó odigó.
Kírios Ne, amesos.
Anna Boró na hrisimopiso to tilefonó sas?
Kírios Ne, efharistos.

to tilefonikó katálogo telephone directory
o hrisós odigós yellow pages

3 *This little girl wants to make a call from the newsstand*

Vaso Er, kírie, boró na tilefoniso?
Kírios Efharistos despinís, peraste.

1 ♦ **thelo na tilefoniso** I want to phone.

iparhi edó kondá? is there near here?

períptero i tilefonikós thálamos a newsstand or a telephone booth.

ine ligo pió kato apó'do it's a little further on (lit. it's a little more down from here). **Apo'dó = apó edó.**

olo efthia tha pate you should go straight ahead (lit. all straight ahead you will go).

2 **tha ithela ke to hrisó odigó** I'd like the yellow pages too. **Hrisós-i-o** literally means 'gold, golden'. You have met **o odigós** meaning 'driver', it also means 'guide'.

boró na hrisimopiso to tilefonó sas? may I use your telephone?

3 ♦ **boró na tilefoniso?** may I telephone? Here is another very useful question involving the use of the telephone, **boró na tilefoniso sto eksoterikó?** (can I call abroad?). The reply could be **ohi, to tiléfono ine mono topikó** (the telephone is only for local calls) or **ne peraste** yes, go ahead.

4 *Where can the boy make a phone call from?*

Pedí Pou boró na tilefoniso?
Kiria Sto proto períptero pou fénete apó edó.
Pedí Efharistó.

5 *Yiorgos is calling Viky from the airport*

Viky Embrós.
Yiorgos Yiá sou Viky, ime o Yiorgos.
Viky Yiá sou Yiorgo ti nea?
Yiorgos Típota idiétero.
Viky Apó pou me pernis?
Yiorgos Apó to aerodrómio.
Viky Yiatí?
Yiorgos Yiatí pame sti Mykono.
Viky Ah! emís pígame hthes. Itan para polí orea.
Yiorgos Se afino Viky yiatí to aeroplano mou fevyi se mia ora.
Viky Endaksi, kaló taksidi ke heretísmata sti yineka sou ke sta pediá.
Yiorgos Yiá sou. Efharistó.

6 *Sometimes you have to spell your name and the name of the hotel*

Yiorgos Embrós!
Vivi Thelo na kliso dio thesis yiá ti Mykono.
Yiorgos Apó pou me pérnete?
Vivi Apó to ksenodohio ARION.
Yiorgos Arion me alfa?
Vivi Ne, alfa, ro, iota, ómikron, ni, sti Glyfada.
Yiorgos Endaksi, ti ónoma?
Vivi Kírios ke kiria Tailor.
Yiorgos Pos to gráfete?
Vivi Taf, alfa, iota, lamda, ómikron, ro, Tailor.
Yiorgos Endaksi, efharistó.

4 ♦ **pou boró na tilefoniso?** where can I phone? Do you remember **pou boró na alakso lires?** (where can I change pounds?).

sto proto períptero at the first newsstand.

pou fénete apó edó which you can see from here (lit. which appears from here).

5 ♦ **embrós** hello! (lit. forward). You can also use **embrós** for 'come in!'

ime o Yiorgos it's Yiorgos. In Greek you say 'I'm Yiorgos' rather than 'it's Maria' when on the phone.

♦ **ti nea?** what's new? (lit. what news?).

apó pou me pernis? where are you calling from? (lit. from where are you taking me?). **Perno tiléfono** is one way of saying 'I'm phoning'.

♦ **emís pígame hthes** *we* went yesterday. **Pígame** is the past tense of **pame**. There is more about forming the past tense of verbs in Unit 14.

se afino I'd better go (lit. I leave you).

♦ **kaló taksidi** bon voyage or good trip. Some other examples: **kalí óreksi** (bon appétit or good appetite) and **kalí epitihia** (good luck).

heretísmata sti yineka sou ke sta pediá greetings to your wife and the children.

6 **thelo na kliso** I want to book.

apó pou me pérnete? where are you calling me from?

♦ **pos to gráfete?** how do you spell it? (lit. how do you write it?)

	7	*A child is reciting the alphabet*

Ena pedí   Alfa
vita
gama
delta
épsilon
zita
ita
thita
yiota
kapa
lamda
mi
ni
ksi
ómikron
pi
ro
sigma
taf
ípsilon
fi
hi
psi
ke omega

Kírios Manolis   Bravo! bravo! . . . bravo!

7 Make sure you know the equivalent sounds in English of all the letters of
the Greek alphabet.

A α	'a' as in father
B β	'v' as in van
Γ γ	'g' as in guild, 'y' as in yet (before 'e' and 'i')
Δ δ	'd' as in door
E ε	'e' as in let
Z ζ	'z' as in zoo
H η	'i' as in police
Θ θ	'th' as in this
I ι	'i' as in police
K κ	'k' as in key
Λ λ	'l' as in live
M μ	'm' as in my
N ν	'n' as in never
Ξ ξ	'ks' as in tricks
O o	'o' as in hot
Π π	'p' as in pie
P ρ	'r' as in red
Σ σ ς★	's' as in send
T τ	't' as in tip
Y υ	'i' as in police
Φ φ	'f' as in four
X χ	'ch' as in Bach or, if you can't make this sound, 'h' as in help
Ψ ψ	'ps' as in tops
Ω ω	'o' as in hot

★ only at the end of words

Note that H η, I ι and Y υ are all pronounced 'i' as in police and O o and
Ω ω are both pronounced 'o' as in hot.

Key words and phrases

To learn

iparhi edó kondá períptero?
pou boró na tilefoniso?
boró na tilefoniso?
sto eksoterikó

is there a newsstand near here?
where can I telephone?
may I telephone?
abroad

To understand

embrós!

hello, come in!

se perno apó to aerodrómio
    to períptero
to tiléfono ine mono yiá topikó

I'm calling you from the airport
    the newsstand
the phone is only for local calls

pos to gráfete?
pígame hthes

how do you spell it?
we went yesterday

kalí óreksi
kaló taksidi

bon appétit, good appetite
bon voyage, good trip

Practice what you have learned

Remember to read through the introduction to each exercise in turn before switching on the tape.

1 Here is part of a telephone conversation. Listen to all of it on the tape and then fill in the gaps from the words below.

Petros	....
Eleni	Yiá sou ...., edó i ....
Petros	Yiá sou, ti ....?
Eleni	.... idiétero.
Petros	Apó pou me ....?
Eleni	Apó to ....
Petros	Pame sto .... apopse?
Eleni	....
Petros	Stis ....
Eleni	Malista.

októ Petro theatro endaksi períptero

Eleni pernis típota nea embrós

2 Here are the names of some of the letters of the Greek alphabet. Follow the example and write out what they are and their names in Roman letters. Check your answers with the tape.

	Letter	Name		Letter	Name
ἄλφα	A α		ρό		
γάμα			σίγμα		
δέλτα			ὔψιλον		
ζῆτα			χί		
κάπα			ψί		
μί			ὠμέγα		

3 You will hear some names spelled out letter by letter in Greek. Listen to the tape and, following the example, write out the name in Roman letters. (Answers p. 186)

a. Ἑ λ έ ν η   *Eleni* ....

b. ῎Α ν ν α ....

c. Π έ τ ρ ο ς ....

d. Γ ι ά ν ν η ς ....

e. Μ α ρ ί ν α ....

f. Μ α ν ώ λ η ς ....

g. Κ ώ σ τ α ς ....

h. Μ ε λ ί σ σ α ....

i. Χ ρ ι σ τ ί ν α ....

j. Γ ε ώ ρ γ ι ο ς ....

Grammar

Making the past tense

In Greek, as in English, there are a number of tenses indicating the past e.g. I was saying, I said, I had said etc. This section will deal with the most common form of the past, the simple past i.e. I said. To make the past tense from the present tense you have to:
1. change the endings
2. move the stress back
For some verbs you also have to:
3. add 'e' or 'i' to the beginning of the verb (this only happens with short verbs)
4. change the stem (main part) of the verb.

For example

present		past	
thel**o**	I want	**í**thel**a**	I wanted
thel**is**	you want	**í**thel**es**	you wanted
thel**i**	he/she/it wants	**í**thel**e**	he/she/it wanted
thél**oume**	we want	thél**ame**	we wanted
thél**ete**	you want	thél**ate**	you wanted
thél**oune**	they want	thél**ane**	they wanted

present		past	
pian**o**	I take	**é**pias**a**	I took
pian**is**	you take	**é**pias**es**	you took
pian**i**	he/she/it takes	**é**pias**e**	he/she/it took
pián**oume**	we take	piás**ame**	we took
pián**ete**	you take	piás**ate**	you took
pián**oune**	they take	piás**ane**	we took

Note the change of stem.

present		past	
mil**ó**	I speak	**mí**lis**a**	I spoke
mil**ás**	you speak	**mí**lis**es**	you spoke
mil**á**	he/she/it speaks	**mí**lis**e**	he/she/it spoke
mil**ame**	we speak	milís**ame**	we spoke
mil**ate**	you speak	milís**ate**	you spoke
mil**ane**	they speak	milís**ane**	they spoke

Note the change of stem

Learn the past tense of these three verbs and make sure you can recognize past endings. In Unit 14 you will find the past tense of **ime** (I am) and **eho** (I have) and the past forms of some other useful verbs.

The Greek alphabet

Combinations of letters

You have now come across all the letters of the Greek alphabet (see p. 179). However, you will need to be able to recognize certain combinations of letters and know how to pronounce them. Study the following list.

αι   'e' as in let
| καιρός | kerós | weather |
| καί | ke | and |

αυ   'av' as in have
| αὔριο | ávrio | tomorrow |
| Αὔγουστος | Ávgoustos | August |

but sometimes 'af' as in after
| αὐτό | aftó | this |

ει   'i' as in police
| τρεῖς | tris | three |
| εἶναι | ine | he/she/it is, they are |

ευ   'ev' as in event
| Εὐρώπη | Evropi | Europe |
| εὐγενικός | evyenikós | polite |

but sometimes 'ef' as in effort
| εὐχαριστῶ | efharistó | thank you |

οι   'i' as in police
| κοινός | kinós | public |
| οἰκονομία | ikonomia | economy |

ου   'oo' as in fool
| μπουκάλι | boukali | bottle |
| οὔζο | ouzo | ouzo |

γγ   'ng' as in angle
| Ἀγγλία | Anglia | England |
| ἄγγελος | ángelos | angel |

γκ   'g' as in get
| γκαρσόν | garsón | waiter |

but in the middle of a word 'ng' as in angle
| ἄγκυρα | ángira | anchor |

γχ   'nh' as in enhance
| με συγχωρεῖτε | me sinhorite | excuse me |

μπ   'b' as in bar
| μπάνιο | bánio | bath, bathe |
| μπλέ | ble | blue |

but in the middle of a word sometimes 'mb' as in limbo
| λάμπα | lamba | lamp |

ντ   'd' as in dot
| ντομάτα | domata | tomato |
| ντούς | dous | shower |

Accents

Note that the ` ´ ` used when a word begins with a vowel have no effect on pronunciation. The three marks ` ´ ` ` ` ` ˜ ` all show on which syllable the word is stressed and nothing else.

Did you know?

The Peloponnese

From Athens one enters the Peloponnese by crossing the road or rail bridges which span the Corinth Canal. The canal, which was planned in ancient times (when mariners were reduced to dragging their ships over the land of the narrow isthmus in order to avail themselves of this 'short-cut'), was finally completed in 1890. However, the ancient remains which lie across the canal bear ample witness to magnificent feats of engineering in other fields. Within a very small area there is Agamemnon's city of **Mycenae** with its imposing Lion Gate and giant beehive tombs, the cyclopean fortress of **Tyrins** and the amphitheatre at **Epidaurus** where the perfect acoustics make it possible for spectators fifty rows back to hear the actors with crystal clarity.

The main town of this region is Nafplion which was the first capital of Greece after the Greek War of Independence in the 1820's. Nafplion has retained much of its nineteenth century charm: the atmosphere of the town is generally convivial and there are excellent fish restaurants where one can enjoy a leisurely meal. Further south there is another town with an agreeable nineteenth-century centre, Sparta. Hardly any traces remain of the ancient city of Sparta, not least because the Spartans themselves were more interested in military than architectural glory. However, at the edge of the plain on which the new town lies, on the slopes of Mt. Taiyetos, there are the remains of **Mistra** where the last Byzantine rulers took refuge after the fall of Constantinople to the Turks in 1453. The Mani – the middle prong of the three peninsulae at the far south of the Peloponnese – is interesting both physically and historically. The lower part of the peninsula is virtually devoid of any vegetation and the landscape almost lunar. Such was the competition for survival in the years before independence that the inhabitants were in a constant state of civil war: village against village and even neighbour against neighbour in the same village. Consequently, Maniot families built themselves tall stone towers. Although the region is now very sparsely populated these extraordinary towers survive.

Your turn to speak

Here you're going to practice asking where you can make a long-distance telephone call and play a vocabulary-building game. Remember to read through the introduction and then work with the tape alone. Alexandros will help you.

1 You are in the street and you want to make a telephone call to England but where is the newsstand?

2 This is 'Kim's game'. Memorize what's on the table, cover up the drawing and answer the questions. You will practice
mikró small
megalo large
ellinikó Greek
angliló English

Answers

14 Talking about the past

You will learn

- to understand questions and statements in the past
- to talk about what happened yesterday
- to use a variety of verbs and phrases in the past
- to answer questions about what happened yesterday

Before you begin

Follow the pattern of study set out below, concentrating on the way people ask and answer questions in the past.

Study guide

	Dialogues 1, 2: listen without the book
	Dialogues 1, 2: listen, read and study the notes
	Dialogues 3, 4: listen without the book
	Dialogues 3, 4: listen, read and study the notes
	Dialogues 5, 6: listen without the book
	Dialogues 5, 6: listen, read and study the notes
	Study *Key words and phrases*
	Complete the exercises in *Practice what you have learned*
	Study *Grammar* and do the exercise
	Do *The Greek alphabet – review*
	Read *Did you know?*
	Do the taped exercises in *Your turn to speak*
	Finally, listen to all the dialogues again

Dialogues

1 *Two friends are trying to remember what they did yesterday*

Katerina Esi thimase katholou ti ékanes ehthés?

Maria Egó ehthés ékana diáfores douliés sto spiti, skáliksa ligo ton kipo ke metá mayírepsa yiá to mesimeri.

Katerina Ah! Er, to apóyevma vyikes katholou ekso?

Maria Káthisa ligo ke ksekourástika ke metá piga stin ksadelfi mou.

Katerina Egó to apóvgema anévika apó ta skaliá sto Likavito, et, ke káthisa ston ílio ke metá katévika kato me to teleferík, ke to vradi vyika pali ekso, ke piga se mia taverna stin Plaka, ákousa bouzouki ke tragoúdia elliniká, fágame kalá ke diaskedásame polí.

1 ♦ **esí thimase katholou ti ékanes ehthés?** do you remember at all what you did yesterday? Other phrases using **thimame** (I remember): **thimame polí kalá** (I remember very well) and **me thimase?** (do you remember me?). **Ékanes** (you did) from **kano** (I do). This is the past tense. You will find other verbs in the past in *Grammar*.

♦ **ehthés** (or **hthés**) yesterday. Other useful words are **prohthés** (the day before yesterday), **i perasmeni evdomada** (last week), **to perasmeno mina** (last month) and **persi** (last year).

♦ **egó (hthés) ékana diáfores douliés sto spiti** I did different jobs in the house yesterday. Remember that you only use the word **egó** for emphasis.

skáliksa ligo ton kipo I dug (around) the garden a little. **Skáliksa** (I dug) from **skalizo** (I dig).

mayírepsa yiá to mesimeri I cooked for midday. **Mayírepsa** (I cooked) from **mayirevo** (I cook).

to apóyevma vyikes katholou ékso? in the afternoon did you go out at all? **Vyikes** (you went out) from **vyeno** (I go out).

♦ **káthisa ligo ke ksekourástika** I sat and relaxed for a while. **Káthisa** (I sat) from **káthoume** (I sit). **Kathiste!** (sit down! take a seat!).

piga stin ksadelfi mou I went to my cousin's. **Piga** (I went) from **pao** (I go).

♦ **anévika apó ta skaliá sto Likavito** I went up Likavitos by the steps. **Anévika** (I went up) from **aneveno** (I go up).

káthisa ston ílio I sat in the sun.

♦ **katévika kato me to teleferik** I went down to the funicular. **Katévika** (I went down) from **kateveno** (I go down).

♦ **to vradi vyika pali** I went out again in the evening.

♦ **ákousa bouzouki ke tragoúdia elliniká** I heard bouzouki and Greek songs. **Ákousa** (I heard) from **akoúo** (I hear).

♦ **fágame kalá ke diaskedásame polí** we ate well and we enjoyed ourselves very much. **Fágame** (we ate) from **trogo** (I eat), a very irregular verb.

2 *Tsela wants to know what Anna did yesterday*

Tsela Pes mou, pou ísouna to vradi?
Anna Ah! Hthes iha pai se mia taverna yiá fayitó, me kati filous ke files.
Tsela Megali parea?
Anna Megali.
Tsela Ta pérases orea?
Anna Polí orea.
Tsela Ti fágate?
Anna Eh! fágame diáfora, mezedákia . . . ihe bouzoúkia, er . . .
Tsela Kalí i mousikí?
Anna Polí orea i mousikí.
Tsela Ke hórepses polí?
Anna Arketá.
Tsela Ti horoús?
Anna Eh! zeibékika, elliniká.

3 *Dimitris wants to know the places Katerina visited when she was in London*

Katerina Egó émena ligaki ékso apó to Londino, sto Epsom.
Dimitris Málista. Piá meri éhete episkefthí tou Londinou?
Katerina Den episkéfthika polá meri, er, yiatí iha polí diávasma, otan ímouna ekí, alá piga sto . . . er, stis yéfires pou ehi to Londino ke tis ida, piga stin pinakothiki, episkéfthika meriká mousia, piga se ekino to mousio pou ehi ta kérina omiómata, um. . .
Dimitris Pígate . . . pígate na dite to mousio tis fisikís istorias?
Katerina Ohi, aftó den to eho episkefthí.
Dimitris Hásate.

ligaki a little bit
i pinakothiki art gallery

2

♦ **pes mou** tell me. The polite/plural form is **peste mou.**

♦ **pou ísouna to vradi?** where were you in the evening? **Ísouna** (you were) from **ime** (see *Grammar*).

iha pai I had gone. You could say simply **piga** (I went).

me kati filous ke files with some (male) friends and (female) friends. In the singular these are **enas filos** (a male friend) and **mia fili** (a female friend). If you want to ask 'with whom?' it is **me pión?** presuming it is a man and **me piá?** presuming it is a woman.

megali parea? lots of people? (lit. large party). **I parea** means both 'a party, group' and 'company' e.g. **den piga monos mou, iha parea** (I didn't go alone, I had company).

♦ **ta pérases orea?** did you have a good time? **Pérases** (you passed/spent) from **pernó** (I pass/spend).

fágame diáfora . . . mezedákia we ate various things. . . hors d'oeuvres.

hórepses polí? did you dance a lot? **Hórepses** (you danced) from **horevo** (I dance).

ti houroús? what dances?

zeibékika, elliniká To zeibékiko is a dance from Asia Minor; **elliniká** means here 'traditional Greek dances'.

3

♦ **egó émena ligaki ekso apó to Londino** I stayed a little bit out of London. **Émena** (I was staying) from **meno** (I stay).

piá meri éhete episkefthí tou Londinou? which places have you visited in London? (lit. of L.). In the singular 'which place?, is **pió meros?**

den episkéfthika polá meri I didn't visit many places.

yiatí iha polí diávasma otan ímouna ekí because I had a lot of studying when I was there. For **iha** (I had) and **ímouna** (I was) see *Grammar*.

♦ **alá piga sto. . . stis yéfires** but I went to the bridges. Note how Katerina changes the **sto** to **stis** to agree with the feminine plural of **i yéfira** (bridge).

pou ehi to Londino ke tis ida which there are in London and I saw them (lit. which London has. . .). **Ida** (I saw) from the irregular verb **vlepo** (I see). In **tis ida** the **tis** stands for **tis yéfires** (the bridges). Other examples: **ton ida** (I saw him), **tin ida** (I saw her).

episkéfthika meriká mousia I visited some museums.

♦ **piga se ekino to mousio pou ehi ta kérina omiómata** I went to that museum which has the wax images.

♦ **pígate na dite to mousio tis fisikís istorias?** did you go to see the Natural History Museum?

♦ **hásate** you missed out (lit. you lost).

4 *Yiorgos wants to know why Vivi didn't come to listen to bouzouki music last night*

Vivi   Yiá sou. . .

Yiorgos   Yiá sou. De mou les pou ísouna hthes?

Vivi   Pote? Ti ora?

Yiorgos   Metaksí deka ke dódeka, se periméname na pame yiá bouzoúkia.

Vivi   Ah ne, tora thimame. Iha polí ponokéfalo ke mou ponouse polí i plati apó ton ílio.

Yiorgos   Ke ti ékanes?

Vivi   Pira dio aspirines ke évala mia alifí ke kimíthika amesos.

Yiorgos   Ah éhases. Emís pígame stin Plaka, akoúsame bouzoúkia ke tora mou ponai polí to kefali apó to polí ouzo.

Vivi   Andio ke perastiká sou.

5 *Yiorgos and Viky went shopping yesterday – but in different places*

Yiorgos   Pou ísaste hthes to proí? Sas pira tiléfono dio forés.

Viky   Ehthés piga sta magaziá.

Yiorgos   Ah! k'egó piga sta magaziá, sto Monastiraki, ke agórasa meriká dora yiá tous filous mou.

Viky   Ah! egó piga stin Ermou ke agórasa ena oreo fórema ke ena zevgari papoútsia. Sas árese to Monastiraki?

Yiorgos   Ne, ine para polí oreo, ávrio tha ksanapao yiatí thelo n'agoraso meriká keramiká.

Monastiraki district of Athens with the flea market and craft shops
odós Ermou Ermou Street (mostly dress and shoe shops)

6 *Viky was waiting for Maria but she didn't turn up*

Viky   Lipón Maria, pou ísouna hthes? Se perímena.

Maria   Ah! piga prota sto mousio.

Viky   Ah! k'egó se perímena na pame na psonísoume. Egó piga yiá psónia.

4 ♦ **pou ísouna hthes?** where were you yesterday?

♦ **pote?** when? With the stress on the end **poté** means 'never'.

♦ **se periméname na pame** we were expecting/waiting for you so that we could go. **Perimeno** (I wait/expect).

♦ **tora thimame** now I remember.

iha polí ponokéfalo I had a bad headache. **O ponos** (pain), **to kefali** (head).

mou ponouse polí i plati apó ton ílio my back was hurting me a lot from the sun.

♦ **ti ékanes?** what did you do?

pira dio aspirines ke évala mia alifí ke kimíthika amesos I took two aspirins and put on an ointment and went to sleep right away. **Perno** (I take), **pira** (I took), **vazo** (I put), **évala** (I put), **kimame** (I sleep), **kimíthika** (I slept).

éhases you missed out.

mou ponai polí to kefali apó to polí ouzo my head aches from all the ouzo (lit. my head hurts me a lot from the lots of ouzo).

♦ **perastiká sou** get well soon. You could just say **perastiká**.

5 **sas pira tiléfono dio forés** I phoned twice. Do you remember **perno tiléfono** (I phone) from Unit 13, dialogue 5? 'One time' is **mia forá**.

♦ **sta magaziá** to the shops.

ke agórasa meriká dora yiá tous fílous mou and I bought some presents for my friends. **Agorazo** (I buy), **agórasa** (I bought). **Ena doro** (a present).

ena zevgari papoútsia a pair (of) shoes.

♦ **sas árese?** did you like?

tha ksanapao I will go again. You can add **ksana-** to the beginning of verbs to mean 'again' e.g. **ksanamiló** (I say again). Another way is to put **pali** (again) *after* the verb: **tha pao pali** (I'll go again).

thelo n'agoraso meriká keramiká I want to buy some ceramics.

6 ♦ **lipón Maria, pou ísouna hthes?** so Maria, where were you yesterday?

♦ **se perímena** I was expecting/waiting for you.

piga prota sto mousio I went first to the museum.

k'egó se perímena na pame na psonísoume and *I* was expecting/waiting for you so we could go shopping.

piga yiá psónia I went shopping.

Key words and phrases

To learn

ékana diáfores douliés	I did different jobs
vyika ekso	I went out
anévika	I went up
katévika	I went down
piga se mia taverna	I went to a taverna
sta magaziá	the shops
stin Ellada	Greece
sto mousio	the museum
fágame kalá	we ate well
ákousa mousikí	I heard music
ímouna	I was
iha	I had
ékane polí zesti	It was very hot
me thimase?	do you remember me?
pote?	when?
perastiká	get well soon

To understand

kathiste!	sit down, take a seat!
peste mou	tell me
pou ísouna?	where were you?
ta perásate kalá?	did you have a good time?
sas perímena	I was expecting/waiting for you
tora thimame	now I remember
sas árese?	did you like (it)?
ti ékanes/kánate ehthés?	what did you do yesterday?
prohthes?	the day before yesterday?
tin perasmeni evdomada?	last week?
ton perasmeno mina?	last month?
persi?	last year?
me pión?	with whom (man)?
me piá?	with whom (woman)?
me pioús?	with whom (pl.)?
pou pígate?	where did you go?
ti fágate?	what did you eat?
pígate na dite?	did you go to see?
hásate	you missed out

Practice what you have learned

These exercises focus attention on things that happened in the past.
Remember to read the instructions to each exercise before beginning.

1 Complete the following conversation by looking at Eleni's diary below.
Listen to the tape for the correct version.

Yiannis Ti ora pires to proinó sou?

Eleni Pira to .... mou stis ....

Yiannis Ti ékanes metá?

Eleni Stis .... piga mia ekdromí stin ....

Yiannis Pou pires to mesimerianó sou?

Eleni Pira to .... se mia ....

Yiannis Metá piyes sti thálassa?

Eleni Ohi, piga sta ....

Yiannis Pote piyes sta katastímata?

Eleni Stis ....

Yiannis To vradi ti ékanes?

Eleni Stis .... piga stin ....

2 Complete these sentences using **vyike**, **pire** and **piye** and translate them into English. (Answers p. 200)

a. O Petros .... to proinó stis deka ....

b. I Anna .... sta katastímata stis enea ....

c. I Eleni .... ekso stis dio ....

d. I Sofia egrapse mia karta stis okto ....

e. O Yiannis alakse lires sti mia ....

3 Complete the dialogue looking at the drawings and using the sentences beneath. Listen to the tape for the correct version.

Nina: Pou pígate hthes to vradi?

Petros: ....

Nina: Me pioús pígate?

Petros: ....

Nina: Ti ípiate?

Petros: ....

Nina: Ti kánate?

Petros: ....

me tous filous mou   ípiame ouzo   pígame se mia taverna   horépsame

Grammar

Verbs

Here are some common verbs with irregular past tenses. Spend a little time trying to absorb them. You'll soon get to recognize them when you hear them.

present		*past*	
thelo	I want	**íthela**	I wanted
ksero	I know	**íksera**	I knew
pino	I drink	**ípia**	I drank
nomizo	I think	**nómisa**	I thought
kapnizo	I smoke	**kápnisa**	I smoked
grafo	I write	**égrapsa**	I wrote
doulevo	I work	**doúlepsa**	I worked
horevo	I dance	**hórepsa**	I danced
anigo	I open	**ániksa**	I opened
klino	I close	**éklisa**	I closed
dino	I give	**édosa**	I gave
kano	I do	**ékana**	I did
trogo	I eat	**éfaga**	I ate
fevgo	I leave	**éfiga**	I left
ferno	I bring	**éfera**	I brought
meno	I live, stay	**émina**	I lived/stayed
perimeno	I expect, wait for	**perímena**	I expected, waited for
vyeno	I go out	**vyika**	I went out
leo	I say	**ipa**	I said
pao	I go	**piga**	I went
katalaveno	I understand	**katálava**	I understood
vlepo	I see	**ida**	I saw
perno	I take	**pira**	I took
vazo	I put	**évala**	I put

And last but not least, here are **ime** (I am) and **eho** (I have) in full:

ímouna	I was	**ímaste**	we were
ísouna	you were	**ísaste**	you were
ítane	he/she/it was	**ítane**	they were
iha	I had	**íhame**	we had
ihes	you had	**íhate**	you had
ihe	he/she/it had	**íhane**	they had

Exercise   Put the verbs in brackets in the past. (Answers p. 200)

a. Hthes .... stin Akropoli (pao)

b. .... sti Glyfada hthes to proí (ime)

c. .... stin taverna hthes (trogo)

d. De .... krasí to vradi (thelo)

e. Persi .... to kalokeri sto Londino (meno)

f. .... to poukámiso sto krevvati sou (vazo)

g. Mílise polí grígora ke den .... (katalaveno)

h. Den .... pos ísouna stin Athina (ksero)

The Greek alphabet – review

Shopping

Here are four shops. Below each shop you will find a list of some of the things you could buy there. Translate the lists into English using the spaces provided. (Answers p. 200)

a. κοτόπουλο ....

b. χοιρινό ....

c. ἀρνάκι ....

d. μοσχάρι ....

e. κιμᾶς ....

a. ψωμί ....

b. ψωμάκια ....

c. φραντζόλα ....

d. φρυγανιές ....

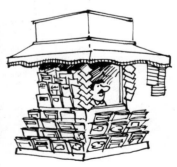

a. ᾿ελιές.........................

b. λάδι ....

c. ρύζι ....

d. φέτα ....

e. ντομάτες ....

a. τσιγάρα ....

b. σπίρτα ....

c. ᾿εφημερίδες.........................

d. περιοδικά ....

e. κάρτες ....

Did you know?

The Ionian Islands and Epirus

The Ionian Islands are both physically and culturally different from the rest of Greece: their vegetation is startlingly lush in contrast to the barren mountain masses of the nearby mainland and their comparative proximity to Italy and long Venetian occupation have given them a strong Italian flavor. Although the islands were a British Protectorate for some fifty years, virtually the only sign of British influence today is the survival of cricket in Corfu.

Corfu is the largest and most popular of the islands; however, despite the extensive exploitation of the coast for tourism, a few miles inland in the mountains rural life is little changed and the village women still wear traditional costumes. The Venetian-style architecture of Corfu town is pleasing and even at the height of summer the place seems to be able to absorb the many visitors without losing its individual atmosphere.

Opposite Corfu there are the imposing mountains of Epirus. The regional capital, Yannina, lies in a valley beside a lake surrounded by steep mountain slopes. It was here that the notorious Ali Pasha defied the Ottoman Sultan at the beginning of the last century and for many years ruthlessly governed a private kingdom. Even today Ali Pasha is a familiar figure in local demonology and his deeds live on in folksongs. Indeed, Epirus is generally famous for its remarkable vocal and instrumental traditional music. Many of the musicians are gypsies, who are very numerous in this part of the country.

South of Yannina there is an ancient amphitheatre at **Dodoni** in a stunning natural setting. As the road continues south it passes through wide plains at the foot of the mountains where tobacco is grown. At the little town of Arta the road goes by the old stone Bridge of Arta. According to legend, when the bridge was built it collapsed every time it was completed. Finally, the Master Mason was told in a dream that it would never stand unless his wife was buried in the foundations. This was duly done and the bridge has stood as firm as a rock ever since. . .

Your turn to speak

Here are two conversations where you can practice talking about something in the past tense. You will use **piga** (I went) and **pígame** (we went). Remember to listen for the prompt before attempting to answer the questions.

1 Back at school after your trip, you have a chat with your Greek teacher.

2 On your flight back you meet the Greek girl who sat next to you on the plane on the way over to Greece.

Answers

Practice what you have learned p. 196 Exercise 2 (a) Petros had breakfast at ten (b) Anna went to the shops at nine (c) Eleni went out at two.

Grammar p. 197 (a) piga (b) ímouna (c) éfaga (d) íthela (e) émina (f) évala (g) katálava (h) íksera.

Τne Greek alphabet – review p. 198 Butcher shop (a) kotópoulo, chicken (b) hirinó, pork (c) arnaki, lamb (d) moshari, beef (e) kimá, mincemeat. Bakery (a) psomí, bread (b) psomákia, rolls (c) frantzola, French bread (d) friganiés, continental-style toast. Grocery (a) eliés, olives (b) ladi, oil (c) rizi, rice (d) feta, white cheese (e) domates, tomatoes. Newsstand (a) tsigara, cigarettes (b) spirta, matches (c) efimerides, newspapers (d) periodiká, magazines (e) kartes, postcards.

15 Stating your intentions

You will learn

- to understand questions and statements in the future
- to talk about your own future plans
- to use nouns and verbs to express the future

Do you remember?

what did you do yesterday?	**ti kánate ehthés?**
where did you go?	**pou pígate?**
do you like Greece?	**sas aresi i Ellada?**
I like Greece very much	**mou aresi polí i Ellada**

Before you begin

You should be able to recognize most of the vocabulary by now, so try to concentrate on the way people talk about the future. Follow the study pattern as usual.

Study guide

Dialogues 1, 2: listen without the book
Dialogues 1, 2: listen, read and study one by one
Dialogues 3, 4: listen without the book
Dialogues 3, 4: listen, read and study one by one
Dialogues 5, 6: listen without the book
Dialogues 5, 6: listen, read and study the notes
Study *Key words and phrases*
Complete the exercises in *Practice what you have learned*
Study *Grammar* and do the exercises
Do *The Greek alphabet – review*
Read *Did you know?*
Do the taped exercises in *Your turn to speak*
Listen to all the dialogues again
Finally, do *Revision/Review Units 13–15* at the end of the book

Dialogues

1 *Anna would like to know what Lakis is going to do tomorrow*

Anna	De mou les ti tha kanis ávrio to proí?
Lakis	Tha pao sti thálassa. Esís?
Anna	Egó, tha pao ekdromí.

2 *Eleni and Anna are making plans for next month*

Eleni	Ti tha kanis ton alo mina?
Anna	Tha pao stin Anglia, ena taksidi.
Eleni	Sou aresi i Anglia?
Anna	M'aresi polí.

to taksidi journey

3 *Dimitris and Katerina are discussing plans for the following day*

Dimitris	Ti tha kánoume ávrio?
Katerina	Ávrio tha pame to proí sti thálassa, ke tha kánoume bánio.
Dimitris	Metá apó to bánio ti alo tha kánoume?
Katerina	Metá tha pame se kanena estiatório ke tha fame. Mou ípan oti, er, se aftó to estiatório, apénandi apó to ksenodohio mas, tha ehi polí kaló psari.

4 *Where shall we go tomorrow?*

Anna	Pou tha pame ávrio to proí?
Lakis	Tha pame stous Delfoús.
Anna	Oréa.

1 ♦ **ti tha kanis ávrio to proí?** what will you do tomorrow morning. You use **tha** + the verb, to make a future sentence, see *Grammar*. Other examples: **tha pao stin Ellada** (I'll go to Greece), **tha pame stin Anglia** (we'll go to England), **pou tha pate?** (where will you go?). Some useful words: **ávrio** (tomorrow), **metá/ístera** (after), **methávrio** (the day after tomorrow), **tou hronou** (next year).

♦ **tha pao sti thálassa** I'll go to the sea. Remember **i thálassa** (the sea) but **sti thálassa** (to the sea).

♦ **tha pao ekdromí** I'll go on an excursion. More examples with **tha: tha pió krasí** (I'll drink wine), and **tha pame sto Londino** (we'll go to London).

2 ♦ **ti tha kanis ton alo mina?** what will you do next month? (lit. what will you do the other month?).

♦ **tha pao stin Anglia** I'll go to England.

3 ♦ **ti tha kánoume ávrio?** what shall we do tomorrow?

tha pame to proí sti thálassa we'll go in the morning to the sea.

tha kánoume bánio we'll have a swim. Remember that you can use **bánio** for a swim or for a bath.

tha pame se kanena estiatório ke tha fame we'll go to a (some) restaurant and we'll eat.

mou ípane oti they told me that. . . The other common word for 'that' is **pos** e.g. **mou ípane pos tha fígoune** (they told me that they will go).

tha ehi polí kaló psari it will have very good fish.

4 **pou tha pame ávrio?** where will we go tomorrow?

♦ **tha pame stoús Delfoús** we'll go to Delfi. Some place names in Greece are plural: Delfi is masculine plural in Greek **i Delfi**, but after **se** (to/in) the masculine plural **i** becomes **tous** and the noun changes its ending to **-ous**.

5 *What about this year's vacation?*

Katerina De mou les Maria, pou tha pame fetos yiá diakopés?

Maria Na sou po, egó tha thelo na pao sta Kalavrita yiatí thelo na anevo me to sideródromo sto monastiri apano, yiá na to do.

Katerina Ne, alá de tha ine ligaki kourastikó na pame toso makriá ke na ímaste makriá apó thálassa yiá to kalokeri?

Maria Oposdípote ine aftó ena próvlima, esí pou tha éleyes?

Katerina Egó tha'thela na pame se ena nisí, ke nomizo oti i Kriti ine to kalítero. Er, mou ípan oti ehi polés periohés, er, yiá na doume, ehi orées akroyialiés ke tha'thela na episkefthoume ke ta Matala, pou ehi 'hippies' ekí, ménoun i 'hippies'.

to monastiri monastery
apano above
oposdípote certainly, anyway
to próvlima problem
to nisí island
i periohés regions
i akroyialiés seashore

6 *Viky and Yiorgos are looking at their horoscopes*

Yiorgos Viky ti mera yeníthikes?

Viky Stis eftá Iouniou, ime dídimos.

Yiorgos Ela na sou diavaso to oroskopió sou, thelis?

Viky Ne, vévea.

Yiorgos Aftí tin evdomada tha lavis leftá, tha ehis polí tihi stin agapi ke tha prepi na prosehis polí to stomahi sou.

Viky Orea. K'esí pote yeníthikes?

Yiorgos Stis deka enea Fevrariou, ime ihthís.

Viky To dikó sou lei: de tha ehis polí tihi me tis douliés sou, tha sou parousiastí ena embódio ke tha gnorisis ena kenoúrio prósopo. Tha ksodepsis de polá leftá.

Dídimos Gemini
Ihthís Pisces

Δίδυμοι   Ιχθύες

(22 Μαΐου – 21 Ιουν.)   (19 Φεβρ. – 20 Μαρ.)

Ερμής   Ποσειδώνας και Δίας

5 ♦ **pou tha pame fetos yiá diakopés?** where shall we go this year on vacation? (lit. for vacations). Remember this useful set of words: **périsi** (last year), **fetos** (this year) and **tou hronou** (next year).

na sou po let me tell you. This is a common reply to questions beginning **de mou les/lete.**

yiatí thelo na anevo me to sideródromo because I want to go up by train.

yiá na to do in order to see it.

de tha ine ligaki kourastikó na pame toso makriá? won't it be a little bit tiring for us to go so far?

ke na ímaste makriá apó thálassa yiá to kalokeri and for us to be far from the sea for the summer.

pou tha éleyes? where would you say?

♦ **tha íthela na pame** I'd like us to go.

nomizo oti i Kriti ine to kalítero I think that Crete is the best.

yiá na doume for us to see. As a question: **yiá na doume?** (may we see?).

thá'thela na episkefthoume ke ta Matala I'd like us to visit Matala too.

6 **ti mera yeníthikes?** what day were you born?

ela na sou diavaso to oroskipió sou come on, let me read you your horoscope.

thelis? would you like me to? (lit. you want?).

tha lavis leftá you will receive money. **Lamvano** (I receive, get), **tha lavo** (I shall receive, get).

tha ehis polí tihi stin agapi you will have a lot of luck in love. **Kalí tihi** is 'good luck!'

tha prepi na prosehis polí to stomahi sou you must take (great) care of your stomach.

to dikó sou lei your's (horoscope) says.

tha sou parousiastí ena embódio an obstacle will appear to you.

tha gnorisis ena kenoúrio prósopo you will get to know a new person. **Gnorizo** (I get to know), **tha gnoriso** (I'll get to know), **gnórisa** (I got to know).

tha ksodepsis de polá leftá you will spend a lot of money too. The **de** here is not **de(n)** 'not', this **de** means 'and, too' and *follows* the verb.

Key words and phrases

To learn

tha pao stin Ellada	I'll go to Greece
stin Anglia	England
stin Athina	Athens
sto Londino	London
sti thálassa	the sea

tha pao mia ekdromí	I'll go on an excursion
tha thelo na pao	I'll want to go
tha pame stin taverna	we'll go to the taverna
tha íthela na pao	I'd like to go

ávrio	tomorrow
methávrio	the day after tomorrow

ton alo mina	next month
tou hronou	next year

ti tha kánoume?	what shall we do?
pou tha pame?	where shall we go?
pou thélete na pame?	where would you like us to go?
pou tha pate yiá diakopés?	where are you going on vacation?

Practice what you have learned

In this section you will be asked to recognize some phrases in the future. As usual you should read the instructions to each exercise before attempting it.

1 Tick the correct answer to the following questions and then check with the tape.

1 Pou tha pate ávrio to proí?
- [ ] ávrio to proí tha pao sti thálassa
- [ ] pao sti thálassa
- [ ] piga sti thálassa

2 Ti tha fame to vradi?
- [ ] tha fame souvlákia
- [ ] tha fao souvlákia
- [ ] tha fai souvlákia

3 Pou tha aláksete ta dollária?
- [ ] álaksa ta dollária stin trápeza
- [ ] tha alakso ta dollária stin trápeza
- [ ] álazo ta dollária stin trápeza

4 Ti ora tha fiyi to plio?
- [ ] to plio tha fiyi stis dódeka
- [ ] to plio éfiye stis dódeka
- [ ] fevyi stis dódeka

2 Answer the following questions using the words in parentheses as in the example. Check your answers on the tape.

Pote tha pate stin Ellada? (avrio to proí)

Tha pao stin Ellada ávrio to proí

Pote tha grápsete mia karta? (ávrio)

....

Pote tha mayirépsete mousaká? (tin ali evdomada)

....

Pote tha pate stin Anglia? (tou hronou)

....

Pote tha horépsete? (to vradi)

....

Pote tha anevite sto Likavito?   (ávrio to apóyevma)

....

Pote tha kánete mia ekdromi?   (to kalokeri)

....

Pote tha fiyi to plio?   (to Savato)

....

3 In each of Yiorgo's answers the words are in the wrong order. Put them in
the right order and check your answers with the tape.

Sofia De mou les Yiorgo pou tha pame fetos yiá diakopés?

Yiorgos Stin Athina na sou po thelo ta pao na egó

....

Sofia De mou aresi i Athina to kalokeri

Yiorgos Pou na esí eleyes pame tha?

....

Sofia Egó tha íthela na pame se ena nisí, ke nomizo oti i Idra ine to

kalítero

Yiorgos oti ine kalítero yiatí nomizis to?

....

Sofia Yiatí ine polí mikró ke ehi orees akroyialiés

Yiorgos pame endaksi

....

Grammar

Expressing the future

The simplest way of expressing the future is by putting **tha** in front of the verb. For example,

kano (I do, make)

tha kano	I will do	**tha kánoume**	we will do
tha kanis	you will do	**tha kánete**	you will do
tha kani	he/she/it will do	**tha kánoune**	they will do

Exercise 1 Translate these future sentences into English. (Answers p. 212)

a. I Anna tha pai stin Anglia ....

b. Tha pame sti thálassa ávrio to proí ....

c. Tha alakso lires metá to proinó ....

d. Methávrio tha ímaste stin Ellada ....

e. Tora tha milame elliniká ....

f. Tou hronou tha eho tris evdomades yiá diakopés ....

g. Ti tha kánete sto Londino? ....

h. Pote tha pate? ....

Negative + tha

If you want to make a future verb negative you put **de** *before* the **tha** e.g. **tha pao** (I will go), **de tha pao** (I will not go).

Exercise 2 Translate these negative future sentences into English. (Answers p. 212)

a. De tha theli kafé símera ....

b. De tha kseri to onomá sas ....

c. De tha pai stin Ameriki horis ti yineka tou ....

d. De tha kani zesti ekí to kalokeri? ....

The Greek alphabet – revision

Hotels and restaurants

You will find below two lists of words which you might want to use in
hotels and restaurants. Translate the lists into English. You might like to
turn to Units 3, 4 and 10 to refresh your memory on some of the words and
also use the vocabulary at the end of the book. (Answers p. 212)

ΞΕΝΟΔΟΧΕΙΟ	HOTEL

ΕΝΟΙΚΙΑΖΟΝΤΑΙ ΔΩΜΑΤΙΑ	ROOMS TO RENT

a. ἕνα ποτήρι ....

b. ἕνα κρεββάτι ....

c. ἕνα σεντόνι ....

d. μία κουβέρτα ....

e. ἕνα μαξιλάρι ....

f. μία πετσέτα ....

g. ἕνα σαπούνι ....

h. ἕνα τασάκι ....

ΤΑΒΕΡΝΑ	ΨΑΡΟΤΑΒΕΡΝΑ
TAVERN	SEAFOOD RESTAURANT

ΕΣΤΙΑΤΟΡΙΟ	ΨΗΣΤΑΡΙΑ
RESTAURANT	GRILL

a. νερό ....

b. ψωμί ....

c. ἁλάτι ....

d. πιπέρι ....

e. κρασί ....

f. χωριάτικη σαλάτα ....

g. μουσακᾶς ....

h. σουβλάκι ....

i. ψάρια ....

j. χαλβᾶς ....

UNIT 15

Did you know?

The Aegean Islands

The Aegean is so dotted with islands that it is almost impossible to travel by sea and lose sight of land. These islands have played a vital role in the economic and cultural life of Greece since ancient times. Now that this part of the country relies so heavily on tourism for its income it is easily forgotten how diverse the activities of the islanders were in the past. While many of the smaller islands survived on fishing and subsistence farming, the larger ones were agricultural producers on quite a large scale. Even archipelagos of small islands like the Cyclades which almost appear too barren to cultivate successfully, produced their own grain – the ghostly lines of disused windmills still bear witness to this. Larger islands like Crete, Lesvos (Mytilini) and Rhodes are still major producers of fruit and vegetables. They still have their specialties: Lesvos, for example, produces the finest ouzo and Crete takes advantage of its warm southern coast to produce winter tomatoes.

Crete is particularly significant in archeological terms – among the many ancient remains there is the Minoan palace at **Knossos,** which was partly restored by the British archeologist Sir Arthur Evans. Rhodes has interesting medieval architecture, most notably the castle of the Knights of St John and the old Turkish quarter (both in the main town).

The proximity of the sea naturally fostered all kinds of maritime activity and, for centuries, many islanders have become traders and merchant seamen. Not surprisingly some became pirates and the depredations of local and foreign privateers are the reason why most old villages are built high above the sea on mountainsides and some are carefully concealed so that they are not easily seen by passing ships. The decline of piracy in the nineteenth century facilitated the expansion of legitimate trade and in our times, of course, Greek shipping activity has spread to the far corners of the globe. Even today the major Greek ship owners are islanders almost to a man.

Your turn to speak

In this section we'll be asking you to take part in two conversations where you can practice expressing the future. Remember to read the introduction to each conversation and then work with the tape alone.

1 You are having a day out with a Greek friend. You want to see as many places as possible. You'll be practicing **tha íthela** (I'd like to. . .) and **tha pame** (we'll go).

2 You want to organize next year's trip with your friend. You'll practice **pou tha pame?** (where shall we go?).

Knossos (Crete)

Revision/Review

Now turn to p. 220 and complete the revision sections on Units 13–15. On the cassette *Revision* follows after this unit.

Answers

Grammar p. 209 Exercise 1 (a) Anna will go to England **(b)** We will go to the sea tomorrow morning **(c)** I will change some pounds after breakfast **(d)** The day after tomorrow we will be in Greece **(e)** Now we will speak Greek **(f)** Next year I will have three weeks for vacation **(g)** What will you do in London? **(h)** When will you go?

p. 209 Exercise 2 (a) He/she won't want coffee today **(b)** He/she won't know your name **(c)** He will not go to America without his wife **(d)** Won't it be hot there in the summer?

The Greek alphabet – review p. 210 Hotels (a) ena potiri, a glass **(b)** ena krevvati, a bed **(c)** ena sendoni, a sheet **(d)** mia kouverta, a blanket **(e)** ena maksilari, a pillow **(f)** mia petseta, a towel **(g)** ena sapouni, soap **(h)** ena tasaki, an ashtray. Restaurants **(a)** neró, water **(b)** psomí, bread **(c)** alati, salt **(d)** piperi, pepper **(e)** krasí, wine **(f)** horiátiki salata, Greek salad **(g)** mousakás, mousaka **(h)** souvlaki, shish kebab **(i)** psária, fish **(j)** halvás, Greek candy.

Revision/Review Units 1–3

Here are some review exercises to remind you of some of the main points of Units 1–3. Exercises 1 and 2 are for listening practice. Exercise 3 will help you to remember the letters of the Greek alphabet you have learned so far and Exercise 4 will give you some practice speaking Greek.

1 Listen to the tape and write in the appropriate greeting for the occasion described in the space provided. (Answers p. 221)

a. You meet some friends at breakfast ..... *Kalimera*
b. You meet a friend at dinner ..... *Kalispepa*
c. You are leaving a party at night ..... *kaliniclata*
d. You want to say 'hello' to a shopkeeper ..... *Ya Sas*

2 Listen to the tape and write in the Greek word for each object in the pictures below. (Answers p. 221)

a. *ma karekla*   **b.** *ena pagoto*

c. *enas kirie Anglos*   **d.** *enas selino*

e. *enas kafes*   **f.** *ena potiri nero*

3 Copy each letter twice.

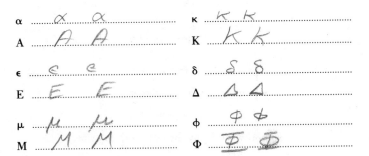

α .... _α_ ..... _α_ .... κ ...... _κ_ .. _κ_ ....

A .... _A_ ...... _A_ .... K ...... _K_ .. _K_ ....

ε .... _ε_ ...... _ε_ .... δ ...... _δ_ ... _δ_ ....

E .... _E_ ...... _E_ .... Δ ...... _Δ_ .. _Δ_ ....

μ .... _μ_ ...... _μ_ .... φ ...... _φ_ .. _φ_ ....

M .... _M_ ..... _M_ .... Φ ...... _Φ_ .. _Φ_ ....

Your turn to speak

4 On the beach. Do this exercise with just the tape.

Revision/Review Units 4–6

1 Follow the clues below and complete the puzzle to find the vertical word.
(Answers p. 221)

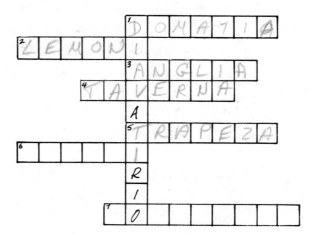

The Greek words for:

1. Where you sleep in a hotel
2. Very bitter fruit
3. England
4. Typical Greek restaurant
5. Where you keep your money
6. Maria has the same mother as you, she is your. . .
7. Fruit, you drink its juice in the morning

2 Complete the following conversation using the words in the box. Listen to the tape to check your answers.

Dina Signomi, parakaló, ...*iparhi*... mia ...*trapeza*... edó kondá?

Lakis Ne, ...*ine*... diakosa ...*metra*... deksiá.

Dina Ti ...*ora*... aniyi?

Lakis ...*stis*... októ.

Dina Ke ti ora ...*klini*...?

Lakis ...*sti*... miámisi.

Dina ...*efharistó*...

Lakis Parakaló.

ine   iparhi   metra   ora   stis   sti   trápeza   efharistó   klini

Your turn to speak

3 You will practice some more numbers and the time.

4 You will practice **pou ine?** and **pió sigá.**

Revision/Review Units 7–9

1 Using **megalos, mikrós, ftinós** and **akrivós** translate the words in parentheses into Greek. Remember to change the ending of these adjectives, if necessary, to agree with feminine or neuter nouns. (Answers p. 221)

a. I (cheap) .... taverna

b. To (big) .... plio

c. To (expensive) .... krasí

d. I (expensive) .... fousta

e. O (big) .... stathmós

f. To (expensive) .... ksenodohio

g. I (small) .... eliá

h. To (small) .... domátio

2 Listen to the tape and write in figures the prices of the cars for rent. (Answers p. 221)

Make of car	Currency	Daily	Per km
Fiat	Drs		
Datsun	Drs		
Opel Ascona	Drs		
Ford Granada	Drs		

Your turn to speak

3 You have decided to go for a picnic so you'll need to go shopping. Afterwards you'll take the bus to Glyfada.

Revision/Review Units 10–12

1 Here is a list of dishes you might find on a Greek menu. Write down each dish in the appropriate section of the menu below and then check your answers on the tape.

arnaki me patates karpouzi feta taramosalata

hirinó me patates domata salata

peponi mila

ohtapodi eliés horiátiki salata kotópoulo me patates

OREKTIKA

PSITA

SALATES

FROUTA

2 Complete this conversation by translating the English answers into Greek. Listen to the tape to check your answers.

Yiannis Sas aresoun ta elliniká fayitá?

Kanela Yes, I like them very much ....

Yiannis Sas aresoun ta psária?

Kanela No, I don't like fish ....

Yiannis Ke o ellinikós kafés?

Kanela I prefer nescafé with milk ....

Yiannis Ti sas aresi na pínete me to fayitó?

Kanela I like to drink red wine ....

Your turn to speak

3 You meet a girl on a bus and want to ask her about herself.

Revision/Review Units 13–15

1 Translate these sentences into English. (Answers p. 221)

a. Piga stin Ellada périsi

....

b. Den katálava, pió sigá parakaló

....

c. Signomi, den sas ida

....

d. Pígame sta magaziá eththés

....

e. Thélame na pame sti thálassa prohthés

....

f. Tha pame sti thálassa ávrio to proí

....

g. Tha kani zesti to kalokeri ekí

....

h. Tha pao sto Londino me to aeroplano

....

i. To garsón tha feri to logariasmó

....

j. Tha pate pió kato ke tha dite to ksenodohio

....

Your turn to speak

2 In this taped exercise you will practice asking questions and expressing the past and the future.

Revision/Review

Answers

Units 1–3 p. 213 Exercise 1 (a) kalimera (b) kalispera (c) kalinihta (d) yiá sas.

p. 213 Exercise 2 (a) mia karekla (b) ena pagotó (c) enas Anglos (d) enas Éllinas (e) enas kafés (f) ena potiri neró.

Units 4–6 p. 215 Exercise 1 (1) domátio (2) lemoni (3) Anglia (4) taverna (5) trápeza (6) adelfí (7) portokali. The word is 'diavatírio'.

Units 7–9 p. 217 Exercise 1 (a) ftiní (b) megalo (c) akrivó (d) akriví (e) megalos (f) akrivó (g) mikrí (h) mikró.

p. 217 Exercise 2 Fiat 350 per day, 5 per km. Datsun 440 per day, 6 per km. Opel Ascona 800 per day, 9 per km. Ford Granada 1,350 per day, 13 per km.

Units 13–15 p. 220 Exercise 1 (a) I went to Greece last year (b) I didn't understand, more slowly please (c) Sorry, I didn't see you (d) We went to the shops yesterday (e) We wanted to go to the sea the day before yesterday (f) We will go to the sea tomorrow morning (g) It will be hot there in the summer (h) I will go to London by plane (i) The waiter will bring the bill (j) You will go further down and you will see the hotel.

Grammar in the course

Grammar summary

For easy reference, the most useful grammar points are set out below

Grammatical terms	*The basic rules*
A VERB denotes action or being, e.g. she *is*, he *eats* mousaka, I *go*	All verbs are given in the first person singular, there is no infinitive form as in English e.g. **thelo** (I want), **kano** (I do).
	Verbs in the *present* tense can be divided into two groups. In the first group the stress is on the next-to-the-last syllable e.g. **katalavéno, dino, doulévo** (Units 1, 11). In the second group the stress is on the last syllable e.g. **miló, kolimbó** (Units 2, 11).
The SUBJECT of the verb is the person or thing who acts or is e.g. *she* goes, *I* am	Personal pronouns (e.g. I, you) are not generally needed before the verb, but they may be used for emphasis. The verb endings indicate who is involved in the action and whether they are singular or plural
	Remember that **kano** can be translated as 'I do' or 'I am doing': there is only one present tense in Greek.
	As well as saying what you are doing, you need to be able to talk about what you have done (in the *past*) and what you are going to do (in the *future*). To form the past tense you usually have to change the present tense in the following ways: by altering the endings, by moving the stress back, by adding either 'e' or 'i' to the beginning of one or two syllable verbs and sometimes by changing the spelling of the stem of the verb (Units 13, 14). To express the future simply place **tha** in front of the verb and add the ending for the person you need, e.g. **tha eho, tha éhoume** (Unit 15).
A NOUN is the name of a person or thing e.g. *Peter, girl, pencil*	All nouns in Greek are either masculine, feminine or neuter. You can usually tell the genders of nouns by their endings. Most masculine singular nouns end in **-os, -as** or **-is**, most feminine nouns in **-i** or **-a** and most neuter nouns in **-o** or **-i** e.g. **andras, yineka, portokali** (Unit 4). The plural form of masculine nouns is **-i** (**stathmós – stathmí**), of feminine nouns **-es** (**yineka – yinekes**) and of neuter nouns **-a** (**domatio – domatia**).
The ARTICLES in English are *the*, *a, an* and *some*.	The word for 'the' is **o** before a masculine singular noun and before a masculine plural one **i**. The word for 'the' before a feminine singular and a feminine plural noun is **i**. The word for 'the' before a neuter singular noun is **to** and before a neuter plural one **ta** e.g. **o andras** **i andres** **i yineka** **i yinekes** **to psomí** **ta psomiá** It is used as in English and *also* before proper names e.g. **o Petros, i Athina**; months of the year **o Aprílios**; days of the week **i Deftera**; and titles like Mr and Mrs **o kírios Petros**. The use of the article in Greek is very important because if left out it changes the meaning of the sentence e.g.

éhete to psomí? (have you got the bread?)
éhete psomí? (have you got some/any bread?)
In other words, if you want to say 'some' or 'any' simply omit the article.
The word for 'a' or 'an' before masculine nouns is **enas**, before feminine nouns **mia** and before neuter nouns **ena** e.g. **enas andras, mia yineka, ena trapezi**. There is no plural form.

An ADJECTIVE describes a noun or a pronoun e.g. *small, red, beautiful*	In Greek, adjectives usually precede the noun with which they 'agree' i.e. an adjective is feminine when describing something feminine and plural when describing something plural. The most common endings are as follows: **-os** for masculine singular **o kalós andras**, **-i** for feminine singular **i kalí yineka** and **-o** for neuter singular **to kaló krasí**. The plural endings are as follows **-i** (m.), **-es** (f.) and **-a** (n.) (Units 7, 8). The words for 'this' and 'that' **aftós-i-o**, and **ekinos-i-o** can be used on their own as in English but when they are used with a noun, the article 'the' has to be included before the noun e.g. **aftós o kafés, ekini i karekla**.
POSSESSIVE ADJECTIVES are words like *my, her, his*	In Greek these words follow the noun e.g. **i karekla <u>mou</u>** (my chair). See p. 129.
An ADVERB describes the way something happens e.g. *well, quickly, beautifully* in 'she reads well', 'she runs quickly' and 'she sings beautifully'	Adverbs are often formed from adjectives e.g. **kalós** (adj.), **kalá** (adv.). **Polí** (very) and **para polí** (very much) are used frequently in Greek.
PREPOSITIONS in English are such words as *near, to, in, into, through, for, with, over*	The most common prepositions in Greek are: **se** (in, into, at), **apó** (from), **me** (with, until), **yiá** (for, to), **horís** (without), **metá** (after) (Unit 10).

Numbers

1	ena	70	evdominda
2	dio	71	evdominda ena
3	tria	72	evdominda dio
4	téssera	73	evdominda tria
5	pende	74	evdominda téssera
6	eksi	75	evdominda pende
7	eftá	76	evdominda eksi
8	októ	77	evdominda eftá
9	enea	78	evdominda októ
10	deka	79	evdominda enea
11	éndeka	80	ogdonda
12	dódeka	81	ogdonda ena
13	dekatria	82	ogdonda dio
14	dekatéssera	83	ogdonda tria
15	dekapende	90	eneninda
16	dekaeksi		
17	dekaeftá	91	eneninda ena
18	dekaoktó	92	eneninda dio
19	dekaenea	93	eneninda tria
20	íkosi	94	eneninda téssera
		95	eneninda pende
21	íkosi ena	96	eneninda eksi
22	íkosi dio	97	eneninda eftá
23	íkosi tria	98	eneninda októ
24	íkosi téssera	99	eneninda enea
25	íkosi pende	100	ekató
26	íkosi eksi		
27	íkosi eftá	101	ekatón ena
28	íkosi októ	102	ekatón dio
29	íkosi enea	200	diakosa
30	trianda	300	trakosa
31	trianda ena	400	tetrakosa
32	trianda dio	500	pendakosa
40	saranda	600	eksakosa
41	saranda ena	700	eftakosa
42	saranda dio	800	oktakosa
50	peninda	900	eneakosa
60	eksinda	1000	hília

Numbers over 100 follow the same order as numbers in English e.g.
150 ekaton peninda
365 trakosa eksinda pende
1,342 hília trakosa saranda dio

Vocabulary

The gender of nouns is indicated in parentheses: masculine (m.), feminine (f.) and neuter (n.). Adjectives are shown with masculine, feminine and neuter endings e.g. **kalós-i-o**. When the forms of verbs which follow **na** and **tha** are listed, you are referred to the present tense for the meaning in English e.g. **paro** see **piano**, (**piano** I take, catch).

adelfí (f.) sister
adelfós (m.) brother
ádia (f.) license, permission
ádia odiyíseos (f.) driver's license
ádios-a-o empty
aerodrómio (n.) airport
aeroplano (n.) plane
aerosinodós (f.) stewardess
afino I leave
aftí-es-a these
aftokínito (n.) car
aftós-i-o he, she, it, this
agorá (f.) market
agórasa I bought
agorazo I buy
agori (m.) boy
akomi more, still, yet
akouo I hear
ákousa I heard
akrivós-i-o expensive
akrivós precisely
akroyiali (n.) seashore
alá but
alakso see **alazo**
alati (n.) salt
alazo I change
alevpi flour
ali-ales-ala other
alifí (f.) ointment
allazo I change
alos-i-o another, other, next
Amerikanida (f.) American woman
Amerikanós (m.) American man
Amerikí (f.) America
amesos at once, immediately
anahórisis (f.) departure
anapsiktikó (n.) drink, refreshment
anaptiras (m.) lighter
andio good-bye
andras (m.) man, husband
aneveno I go up
anévika I went up
Anglia (f.) England
Anglida (f.) Englishwoman
anglika (n.) English language
anglikos-i-o English
Anglos (m.) Englishman
anigo I open
ániksi (f.) spring
aniktós-i-o open
apano above
apénandi facing, across the street
aplós-i-o one-way, simple

apó from, than, of, by
apódiksi (f.) receipt
apola everything, all kinds
apopse tonight
apóyevma (n.) afternoon
Aprílios (m.) April
árese it pleased
aresi it pleases
argótero later
aristerá left
arithmós (m.) number
arketá a fair amount, enough
arnaki (n.) lamb
artopiio (n.) bakery
artopolio (n.) bakery
aspirini (f.) aspirin
aspros-i-o white
astinomia (f.) police
Athina (f.) Athens
átomo (n.) person
avgó (n.) egg
Ávgoustos (m.) August
ávrio tomorrow

bakáliko (n.) grocery store
balkoni (n.) balcony
bánio (n.) bathroom, bath
bar (n.) bar
barbouni (n.) red mullet
bira (f.) beer
ble (n.) blue
blouza (f.) blouse
boró I can
boukali (n.) bottle
brostá forward, in front of

dáktilo (n.) finger
damáskino (n.) plum
daskala (f.) teacher (woman)
dáskalos (m.) teacher (man)
Deftera (f.) Monday
defterólepto (n.) second (time)
défteros-i-o second
deka ten
dekáriko (n.) ten drachma piece
Dekémvrios (m.) December
deksamení (f.) tank
deksiá right
de(n) not (before a verb)
den pirazi it doesn't matter
despinís (f.) Miss
diáforos-i-o different
diakopés (f.) vacation(s)

diakosa two hundred
diaskedásame we enjoyed
diávasma (n.) study
diavatírio (n.) passport
Dídimi Gemini
dikigoros (m.) lawyer
dikós-i-o your
diladí that is to say, in other words
dino I give
dio two
diplós-i-o double
diskoték (f.) disco
distihós unfortunately
do see vlepo
dokimazo I try, taste
dollário (n.) dollar
domata (f.) tomato
domátio (n.) room
dondi (n.) tooth
doro (n.) gift, present
doste mou give me
doulevo I work
douliá (f.) work, job
dous (n.) shower
drahmí (f.) drachma
dromos (m.) road

edó here
édosa I gave
éfaga I ate
efharistó thank you
efharistos gladly
éfhoume I wish
éfiga I left
efimerida (f.) newspaper
efthia straight
eftihia (f.) luck
egó I
Egókeros Capricorn
eho I have
ehthés yesterday
ékana I did
ekató hundred
ekdromí (f.) excursion
ekí there
ekinos-i-o he, she, it, that
eksartate it depends
eksi six
eksinda sixty
ekso out, outside
éksodos (f.) exit
ekosterikó (n.) abroad, exterior
ela come (familiar)
elate come (formal, pl.)
eléftheros-i-o single, free
eliá (f.) olive
Ellada (f.) Greece
Éllinas (m.) Greek man

Ellinida (f.) Greek woman
elliniká (n.) Greek language
ellinikós-i-o Greek
embódio (n.) obstacle
embrós hello, come in
emena me
émena I was living
émina I lived
emís we (emphatic)
ena (n.) one, a, an
enas (m.) a, an
endaksi all right, OK
éndeka eleven
eneninda ninety
enikiaso see enikiázome
enikiázome I rent
eos until
epanalamvano I repeat
epanalavo see epanálamvano
episis also, too
episkefthome I visit
episkéftika I visited
epistrofí (f.) round-trip ticket
eptá seven
érhoume I come
esás you (for emphasis)
esena you (familiar for emphasis)
esí you (familiar)
esís you (formal, plural)
estiatório (n.) restaurant
ethnikós-i-o national
etsi so, like this
etsi ki etsi so so
évala I put
evdomada (f.) week
evgenikós-i-o kind, polite

fame see trogo
farmakio (n.) pharmacy
fayitó (n.) food, meal
ferno I carry, bring
fero see ferno
feta (f.) Greek cheese
fetinós-i-o this year's
fevgo I leave
Fevrouarios (m.) February
fili (f.) friend (woman)
filos (m.) friend (man)
filous (m.) friends
fisikós-i-o natural
forá (f.) time
fórema (n.) dress
fotografia (f.) photograph
fournos (m.) oven, bakery
fousta (f.) skirt
frandzola (f.) French-style loaf
fraulo (n.) strawberry
freskos-i-o fresh

friganiá (f.) toast
frouto (n.) fruit
fthinóporo (n.) autumn

gala (n.) milk
Gallida (f.) Frenchwoman
galliká (n.) French language
Gallós (m.) Frenchman
garsón (m.) waiter
glifó I lick
glikós-i-o sweet
glipso see glifó
gnorizo I know
grafio (n.) office
grafo I write, spell
grammatévs (m/f) secretary
grammatósimo (n.) stamp
grígora fast, quickly

halvás (m.) ·halva
hano I lose
hará (f.) joy
hárika It was nice meeting you
hásate you lost
hérete hallo, good-bye
hérete hello, goodbye
heretísmata (n.) greetings
heró polí pleased to meet you
hília thousand
hiliómetro (n.) kilometer
himonas (m.) winter
hioni (n.) snow
hionizi it snows
hirinó (n.) pork
honaki (n.) cone
hora (f.) country
hórepsa I danced
horevo I dance
horiátiki salata Greek salad
horiátikos-i-o village (adj.)
horió (n.) village
horís without
horós (m.) dance
hrímata (n.) money
hrisimopió I use
hrisimopiso see hrisimopió
hrisós (m.) gold
hroma (n.) color
hronos (m.) time, age
hthes yesterday

i (f.) the
i or
Ianouários (m.) January
ida I saw
idea (f.) idea
idiéteros-i-o special
iha I had

íkosi twenty
ilektrikós-i-o electric
ílios (m.) sun
ime I am
ímouna I was
Ioúlios (m.) July
Iounios (m.) June
ipa I said
ipálilos (m/f.) employee
iparhi there is
ipárhoune there are
ipografo I sign
ipograpste (edó) sign (here)
ipóyio (n.) basement
ísia straight
isitírio (n.) ticket
isos perhaps
isóyio (n.) ground floor
ístera afterwards, later
istoria (f.) history
Italia (f.) Italy
Italida (f.) Italian woman
Italós (m.) Italian man
íthela I wanted

kafenio (n.) café
kafés (m.) coffee
kakao (n.) cocoa
kalá well, all right
kalimera good day
kalinihta good night
kalispera good afternoon
kalíteros-i-o better
kalokeri (n.) summer
kalós-i-o good
kalós orísate welcome
kalós sas vríkame glad to be here
kamia (f.) anyone, no one
kanena (n.) anything, nothing
kanenas (m.) anyone, no one
kano I do, make
kapnizo I smoke
karekla (f.) chair
Karkinos Cancer
karpouzi (n.) watermelon
karta (f.) postcard
katálava I understood
katalaveno I understand
katálogos (m.) menu, list,
   directory
katástima (n.) shop
kateveno I get off, go down
kathe every, each
kathiyitís (m.) professor,
   teacher
kathiyítria (f.) professor,
   teacher
katholou at all, not at all

kati something, anything
kato under, down
ke and, too
kéfali (n.) head
kéndima (n.) embroidery
kenoúrios-a-o new
keramiká (n.) ceramics
kérina of wax
kerós (m.) time, weather
kiló (n.) kilogram
kima (n.) wave
kimame I sleep
kimás (m.) minced meat
kimíthika I slept
kinós-i-o common, public
kipelaki (n.) tub, cup
kipos (m.) garden
kiria (f.) Mrs, woman
Kiriakí (f.) Sunday
kírios (m.) Mr, sir
kítakse! look!
kitazo I look
kitó I look
kítrinos-i-o yellow
klino I close, shut
klistós-i-o closed
kókkinos-i-o red
kolimbó I swim
kondá near
kori (f.) daughter
koritsi (n.) girl
kostoumi (n.) suit
kotópita (f.) chicken pie
kotópoulo (n.) chicken
kourasmenos-i-o tired
koutali (n.) spoon
koutí (n.) box
kouverta (f.) blanket
krasí (n.) wine
kreas (n.) meat
kremidi (n.) onion
kreopolio (n.) butcher shop
krevvati (n.) bed
krima (n.) pity
krio (n.) cold
kriono I am cold
krios-a-o cold
ksadelfi (f.) cousin
ksaná again (added to verbs)
ksekourástika I relaxed
ksenodohio (n.) hotel
ksenodohos (m.) hotel owner
ksero I know
ksidatos-i-o pickled
ksodevo I spend

ladi (n.) oil
lahanaki (n.) cabbage

lamba (f.) lamp
lástiho (n.) tire
laví (n.) handle
leftó (n.) minute (time)
lemonada (f.) lemonade
lemoni (n.) lemon
leo I say
leofório (n.) bus
leoforos (f.) avenue
Leon Leo
leptó (n.) minute (time)
ligaki a little bit
ligos-i-o a little, a bit
lipón then, well then
lipoume I am sorry
logariasmós (m.) bill
Londino (n.) London
loukániko (n.) sausage

ma but
magazí (n.) shop
maheri (n.) knife
Maios (m.) May
makriá far, away, distant
málista yes, certainly
marmelada (f.) jam, marmalade
Mártios (m.) March
mas our, us, to/for us
mayírepsa I cooked
mayirevo I cook
mazí together
me with, until
me (m/f.) me
megalos-i-o large, big
me lene my name is
meli (n.) honey
melidzanosalata (f.) eggplant
   purée
meno I stay, live
mera (f.) day
meri (n.) places
merida (f.) portion
merikí-es-a some
meros (n.) place
mesa inside
mesimeri (n.) midday, noontime
mesimerianó (n.) lunch
me sinhorite excuse me, sorry
metá after
metaksí between, among
métrios medium
metro (n.) meter
méyethos (m.) size
mezés (m.) tidbit
mia (f.) one, a, an
mihanikós-i-o (m.) engineer
mikrós-i-o small
milao I speak

mílisa I spoke
milo (n.) apple
minas (m.) month
mipos I wonder if, perhaps
misós-i-o half
mitera (f.) mother
monastiri (n.) monastery
mono only
monos-i-o alone
moró (n.) baby
mou my, me, for/to me
mou aresi I like (it)
mou lipi I am lacking, short of
mousakás (m.) mousaka
mousiki (f.) music
mousikós (m.) musician
mousio (n.) museum

na to, that, in order to, let, may
na there/here it is!
ne yes
nea (n.) news
Nea Yorky New York
neró (n.) water
nescafé (n.) instant coffee
nisí (n.) island
Noémvrios (m.) November
nomizo I think, believe
nóstimos-i-o tasty, attractive
noúmero (n.) number

o (m.) the
Októvrios (m.) October
odigós (m.) driver, guide
odondókrema (f.) toothpaste
odós (f.) street
ogdonda eighty
ohi no, not
oktapodi (n.) octopus
októ eight
ola mazí altogether
Ollandia (f.) Holland
olos-i-o all
ónoma (n.) name
oposdípote anyway, definitely
ora (f.) time, hour
óreksi (f.) appetite
orektiká (n.) hors d'oeuvres,
    appetizers
oreos-a-o beautiful, lovely
orismeni-es-a certain, some
oriste here it is, here's what you
    want
oriste? what would you like? Pardon?
órofos (m.) floor
os until
otan when
oti that

ouzo (n.) anise-flavored aperitif

pagotó (n.) ice cream
pali again
panda always
pandremenos-i-o married
panepistímio (n.) university
pandeloni (n.) trousers
pao I go
papoútsia (n.) shoes
pará to (time)
para very, too much
parakaló please, don't mention it
paralavo I receive
paralia (f.) waterfront
paramoní (f.) stay
Paraskeví (f.) Friday
paráthiro (n.) window
parea (f.) company, party
paro see piano
parousiazo I present, show
Parthenos Virgo
pastítsio (n.) macaroni pie
patata (f.) potato
pateras (m.) father
patrida (f.) native country
pedí (n.) child
Pempti (f.) Thursday
pendakosa five hundred
pende five
peninda fifty
peponi (n.) melon
pera over, far, on the other side
perasmenos-i-o last
perastiká get well soon
perímena I waited, expected
perimeno I wait, expect
periodikó (n.) magazine
periorhí (f.) region
peripou about
períptero (n.) newsstand
perro/piano I take
persi/périsi last year
perisótero more
pernó I pass
perpató I walk
pes mou tell me
piano/perno I take
piato (n.) plate
piga I went
pikántikos-i-o spicy, hot
pikrós-i-o bitter
pinakothiki (f.) art gallery
pino I drink
pió more
piós-a-o who, which
piperi (n.) pepper
piperiá (f.) green pepper

pirouni (n.) fork
pite see leo
plastikos-i-o plastic
plati (f.) back
platia (f.) square
plaz (f.) beach
plio (n.) boat
plirofories (f.) information
plirono I pay
plírosa I payed
podósfero (n.) soccer
pollá many
polí very, very much
ponai it hurts
ponokéfalos (m.) headache
ponouse it hurt
portokalada (f.) orangeade
portokali (n.) orange
pos that, which
pos? how?
pos certainly, yes
posi-es-a? how many?
posos-i-o? how much?
pote when
poté never
potiri (n.) glass
pou where
poukámiso (n.) shirt
poulman (n.) tour bus
prama (n.) thing
prasinos-i-o green
prepi it is necessary, must
prohoró I go forward
prohthés the day before yesterday
proí (n.) morning
proinó (n.) breakfast
pros to, towards
proseksis be careful
prósopo (n.) first, face, person
prota first of all
protimó I prefer
protos-i-o first
próvlima (n.) problem
psari (n.) fish
psihalizi it is drizzling
psiliká (n.) notions store
psistariá (f.) grill
psitá (n.) roasts, roasted meats
psomaki (n.) roll
psomi (n.) bread
psónia (n.) shopping
psonizo I shop

raketes (f.) racquets
retsina (f.) resinated white wine
rizi (n.) rice
rodákino (n.) peach
roloi (n.) watch, clock

rotó I ask

salata (f.) salad
saranda forty
sas you, to you, for you
sas your
sas aresi you like it
Sávato (n.) Saturday
se you
se to, into, in
sendoni (n.) sheet
Septémvrios (m.) September
serviro I serve
servitora (f.) waitress
sideródromos (m.) railway
sigá slowly
signomi sorry
simera today
simio (n.) point
sinántisi (f.) meeting
sinhoró I pardon, forgive, excuse
sinistó I introduce
sistiso see sinistó
skáliksa I dug
skalizo I dig
sketos-i-o plain, simple
Skórpios Scorpio
Skotia (f.) Scotland
sokolata (f.) chocolate
soupa (f.) soup
souvlaki (n.) kebab
spanakópita (f.) spinach pie
spirta (n.) matches
spiti (n.) house
stamatiso see stamató
stamató I stop
stasi (f.) stop
stathmós (m.) station
stelno I send
stenó (n.) side street
stenós-i-o narrow
sti(n) to/in
stilo see stelno
sto(n) to/in
stomahi (n.) stomach
stripso see strivo
strivo I turn

tahidromio (n.) post office
taksí (n.) taxi
taksidi (n.) trip, journey
taksidiótisa (f.) traveller (woman)
tamias cashier
tamio (n.) teller's window
taramosalata (f.) cod-roe purée
tasaki (n.) ashtray
taverna (f.) tavern
Tavros Taurus

tehni (f.) craft
teleferík (n.) funicular
teloniakós ipálilos (m./f.) customs
  officer
telonio (n.) customs
tessera four
Tetarti (f.) Wednesday
tétarto quarter
tétios-a-o such, similar
tha (word introducing future)
thálamos (m.) newsstand, cabin
thálassa (f.) sea
theatro (n.) theatre
thelo I want
thesi (f.) seat, class
thimame I remember
ti? what?
tiganitós-i-o fried
tiherós-i-o lucky
tihi (f.) luck
tilefoniso see tilefonó
tiléfono (n.) telephone
tilefonó I telephone
tiligo I wrap up, tie
tilikso see tiligo
ti(n) the
tin imera per day
típota any, anything, nothing
típota alo anything else
tirí (n.) cheese
tirópita (f.) cheese pie
Toksotis Sagittarius
to(n) the
tópikos-i-o local
tora now
tosos-i-o so much, so many
tote then
toualeta (f.) toilet
tou hronou next year
touristas (m.) tourist (man)
touristikó grafio (n.) tourist office
tourístria (f.) tourist (women)
tragoúdia (n.) songs
trápeza (f.) bank
trapezi (n.) table
treno (n.) train
tria three
trianda thirty
Triti (f.) Tuesday
tritos-i-o third
tro I eat
trogo I eat
tsai tea
tsigara (n.) cigarettes

valitsa (f.) suitcase
valo see vazo
vamvákeros-i-o cotton
vamvaki (n.) cotton wool
varís-ia-i heavy
vathos (n.) depth, back
vazo I put
venzini (f.) gasoline
veríkoko (n.) apricot
vévea certainly
veveos certainly
vísino (n.) sour cherry
vlepo I see
volta (f.) walk, ride
vourtsa (f.) brush
voútiro (n.) butter
vradi (n.) evening, night
vradinó (n.) dinner, supper
vrastós-i-o boiled
vrehi it rains
vrohí (f.) rain
vyeno I go out
vyika I went out

Walia (f.) Wales

yéfira (f.) bridge
yematos-i-o full
yemizo I fill
yeníthika I was born
Yermania (f.) Germany
Yermanós (m.) German man
yévmata (n.) meals
yiá for
yiá (f.) health
yiá sas hello, goodbye (formal)
yiá sou hello, goodbye (familiar)
yiaourti (n.) yogurt
yiatí why, because
yineka (f.) woman, wife
yiós (m.) son
yiro about, around
yortí (f.) festival, celebration

záhari (f.) sugar
zaharoplastio (n.) pastry shop
zésti (f.) heat
zestós-i-o hot
zevgari (n.) pair
Zigos Libra
zitiso see zitó
zitó I ask for
zoí (f.) life

Index

Notes